The Word of Flux

Modern Man and the Problem of Knowledge

ROUSAS JOHN RUSHDOONY

Ross House BOOKS

VALLECITO, CALIFORNIA

Copyright 1965
Dorothy Rushdoony
and the Rushdoony irrevocable trust

reprinted 2002

Ross House Books
PO Box 67
Vallecito, CA 95251
www.rosshousebooks.org

Library of Congress Control Number: 2002094211
ISBN: 1-879998-31-9

Printed in the United States of America

**Our thanks to those who made
the 2002 reprinting of this book possible.**

Mr. & Mrs. Donald Alexander * Paul T. Bergaus * Clara Bianchi *
Michael & Marian Bowman * James & Judith Bruner *
John & Gloria Buzard * Dennis Clarys * Stephen & Janet Coakley *
Robert & Martha Coie * Kenneth W. Cope *
In Memory of Daniel Oliver Crews *
Richard & Elizabeth Crews * Jon & Patricia Davidson *
Dr. Anne L. Davis * David & Joan Dobert * Justin & Melanie Dock *
Dominion Covenant Church * Colonel & Miriam Doner *
In memory of Louise E. Duntz * John & Joan Dyer *
Rev. Dale Dykema & Reformation Presbyterian Church *
Dr. & Mrs. Nicholas H. Edwards * David & Maurietta Estler *
Harry & Marcella Fagan * Jack R. Faris * Robert & Marisa Frank *
Freedom Baptist Church *Michael & Mary Ann Frodella *
The Craig George Family * Dwight & Kathleen George *
Raphael A. Hanson III * Cathy Harnish * Keith & Antha Harnish *
Rev. & Mrs. Samuel D. Harrison * John William Helm *
William & Ruth Hewson * Dr. & Mrs. Herbert Hopper *
E.L.D.H. in memory of Lee & Thomas * Kenneth & Cindy Ii *
Earl & Dorothea Keener * Douglas Floyd Kelly * John B. King, Jr. *
David & Annie Knowles * Sarah Paris Kraft * Dr. & Mrs. Gary Kunsman *
John & Karen La Fear * Marguerite A. Lane * Dr. & Mrs. J.H. Lawson *
Gary Livingston * In memory of Muril & Florence Lovelace *
Joanna, Rachel & Daniel Manesajian * Steve & Belle Merritt *
Norman Milbank * Clint & Elizabeth Miller * Charles & Alfreida Moore *
Dr. Dean Moore * Timothy Patrick Murray * The Jim Nelson Family *
Dr. Heriberto Ortega * Chris & Anne Passerello *
The Howard Phillips Family * Gavin & Rachel Quill *
Greg Reger & Family * Steven Rogers * Frederic Rothfus *
Levi A. R. Rouse * Rebecca, Jill & Emily Rouse * April Rushdoony *
Terry & Janie Saxon * Virginia Schlueter * Anthony Schwartz *
Ford & Andrea Schwartz * Martin & Darlene Selbrede *
Guy Shea * Keith Shepherd *
SonRise Christian Community Church & Academy *
Phil & Petiflor Speilman * Eileen Stanley * Elmer & Naomi Stolzfus *
Martin Stroub * Scot Sullivan * Steve & Jacque Tanner *
Dr. David & Dorothy Terhune * Don & Betty Thompson *
Harry & Jo Ellen Valentine * Ellen Van Buskirk * Ellen Vasbinder *
Magnus Verbrugge * The Howard Walter Family *
Billie Welch * The Jeff White Family * Allan & Margaret Withington *
Roy S. Wright * David E. Young * Jeff & Cynthia Zylstra

Other books by
Rousas John Rushdoony

The Institutes of Biblical Law, Vol. I
The Institutes of Biblical Law, Vol. II, Law & Society
The Institutes of Biblical Law, Vol. III, The Intent of the Law
Systematic Theology (2 volumes)
Hebrews, James & Jude
The Gospel of John
Romans & Galatians
Thy Kingdom Come
The Death of Meaning
Intellectual Schizophrenia
Foundations of Social Order
The "Atheism" of the Early Church
The Biblical Philosophy of History
The Mythology of Science
This Independent Republic
The Nature of the American System
The Messianic Character of American Education
The Philosophy of the Christian Curriculum
Christianity and the State
Salvation and Godly Rule
God's Plan for Victory
Politics of Guilt and Pity
Roots of Reconstruction
The One and the Many
Revolt Against Maturity
By What Standard?
Law & Liberty

For a complete listing of available books
by Rousas John Rushdoony and other
Christian reconstructionists, contact:

ROSS HOUSE BOOKS
PO Box 67
Vallecito, CA 95251
www.rosshousebooks.org

To Dr. Cornelius Van Til

A Father in the Faith

Table of Contents

Preface

In March, 1973, at the invitation of Dr. Morton H. Smith and the Reformed Theological Seminary, Jackson, Mississippi, I taught a course at the seminary on the philosophy of knowledge, epistemology. Subsequently, with additions, these same lectures were delivered to a Chalcedon adult study group in California. This book is the product of those two series of lectures.

Even a casual glance at the contents of this study makes obvious its indebtedness to the philosophy of Dr. Cornelius Van Til. At Reformed Theological Seminary these lectures were a supplement to the reading of Dr. Van Til's *A Christian Theory of Knowledge* and *A Survey of Christian Epistemology* (first published under the title of *The Metaphysics of Apologetics* in 1932).

I am happy to acknowledge the fact that I am a member of the Van Tilian school of thought. The strength of this study is derived from his position, and its inadequacies are mine. This study is offered as a sidelight on the very important questions of a valid theory of knowledge, and it is my hope that its reading will lead to a study of Van Til's works.

I am grateful to Dr. Smith and the faculty and students of Reformed Theological Seminary for the cordial reception to me and to the lectures.

I am grateful also to James B. Jordan, who typed the manuscript for me.

Rousas John Rushdoony
Chalcedon
1975

1

Facts and Epistemology

Some years ago, while a student at the university, I was studying Berkeley and Hume one evening when a friend stopped by. A.T. had gone directly from high school into business; he was a young man of superior intelligence and a very practical disposition. He asked me, after looking briefly into Berkeley and Hume, "What is this stuff about?" I explained briefly that these two men were philosophers in the school of empiricism, a school which holds that the sole source of all knowledge is experience. By experience these philosophers mean sense experience, all the data which our sense perceptions report to us. George Berkeley (1685-1753) held that our senses bring reports of a world around us to our minds, but we have no direct knowledge of that world or its reality. Berkeley tried to prove the non-existence of an unspiritual, unthinking matter. There is no such thing as a matter substance, only sense impressions. However, our ideas do give us a coherent, orderly, and, somehow, inevitable world. What is the nature of that world? Our ideas require some cause beyond our own will, and obviously, this cause is not unthinking matter. The cause of these ideas is God. God is the objective cause of all sense impressions and gives them an

objective order, validity, and significance. Berkeley thus
concluded, in his *A Treatise on the Principles of Human
Knowledge*, which was published when Berkeley was only
twenty-five, that,

> CXLIX. It is therefore plain, that nothing can be more
> evident to any one that is capable of the least reflection,
> than the existence of God, or a spirit who is intimately
> present to our minds, producing in them all that variety of
> ideas or sensations, which continually affect us, on whom
> we have an absolute and entire dependence, in short, "in
> whom we live, and move, and have our being." That the
> discovery of this great truth which lies so near and obvious
> to the mind, should be attained to by the reason of so very
> few, is a sad instance of the stupidity and inattention of
> men, who, though they are surrounded with such clear
> manifestations of the Deity, are yet so little affected by
> them, that they seem as it were blinded with excess of
> light.[1]

David Hume (1711-1776), I went on to explain, carried the
analysis of knowledge a step further. He declared that the mind
is like a theatre; sense perceptions make their appearance and
pass away. Indeed, the mind is really nothing more than a series
of sense perceptions; we have no idea as to the reality behind
them, or of what material or substance they are made. All we
have are sense perceptions. There is no evidence either for God
or for the reality of a material world. A real and certain
knowledge of the external world is thus impossible.

Immanuel Kant (1724-1804), I added, wanted to preserve
knowledge from the consequences of the work of Berkeley and
Hume. The very real question was: is knowledge possible? The
logical answer was that it was not, and yet men seemed to have
some valid knowledge of the world of nature. For Kant, the
impressions of the world enter our mind and become a part of
it, so that the external world, as we know it, is to a large degree
a construct of our mind and a part of it. We can never know

---

[1] *The Works of George Berkeley* (London: Richard Priestly, 1820), I, 101.

things in themselves. The world as we know it is at least relative to our mind if not a construct made by our mind.

A. T. began to ask a number of very intelligent questions. He was also asking questions designed to fit Berkeley, Hume, and Kant into the world he knew. Were they people like Mary Baker Eddy? Finally, A. T. shook his head in amazement and declared, "They are crazy." These philosophers were smart men, he conceded, and the problem they had raised was an interesting puzzle, but what would ever possess a man to think like that, and to work himself into such an absurd blind alley?

His question was far more to the point than I was able to appreciate at that time. What did possess men to begin as Descartes did and then to pursue a line a reasoning that led to Kant? For the Christian theist, who begins with the Sovereign and Triune God and who thus makes the God of Scripture foundational to all things as the principle of meaning and interpretation, the road taken by modern philosophy is an impossibility. The man, however, who begins with a defective doctrine of God, or who begins with man as ultimate, man as his own god, does have a serious problem. Either God is the source of all possibility, or He is not. If God is the source of all possibility, then God is the source of all knowledge, and He has established the possibility of knowledge and also its validity. However, if God is not the source of all possibility, then knowledge is an extremely difficult problem. How do we know that what we know is valid knowledge, or that valid knowledge exists? A distinguished professor in the graduate school of a major university insisted, in a discussion with me, that most of reality is unknowable because it is irrational and meaningless. However, he held, some knowledge is possible because the universe has a "thin edge" of rationality to it, and this science is trying to grasp. He would not answer the question of the source of this thin edge of rationality. How had universal irrationality and meaninglessness produced his thin edge of rationality? And how could he speak of a universe? To do so was to presume a rational coherence in reality. Why not a multiverse, as some hold? Or, more logically, as we shall see, why not an infinite number of brute facts, all irrational, meaningless, and unrelated one to another? Had he not denied the possibility of any rationality in positing the ultimacy of irrationality? How, out of a vast ocean of irrationality, could a thin edge of reason and order appear? Of course, to maintain the possibility of some kind of knowledge, however meager, it was necessary for him to deny total irrationality and assert instead near total meaninglessness. On the other hand, to assert a total order and rationality in the universe would have been to admit the reality of God, and this he was unwilling to do.

Here then is the reason why men pursue the line of reasoning they do. Knowledge is important to man. To surrender the possibility of knowledge is an abdication of life, of the present and the future. The unregenerate thinker, however, is anxious to command the world and time, not to surrender it. As a result, although his denial of God makes knowledge a major problem, he cannot abandon it without surrendering the very thesis of his revolution, to *know* reality independently of God (Gen. 3:5).

Without knowledge, man is helpless; a man's inability to cope with life is in ratio to his ignorance. While knowledge is not salvation, it is still inseparable from it. If a man is suddenly blinded and then placed in an unfamiliar place and world, he is indeed helpless. His helplessness is even greater if we assume that, with his blinding, all previous knowledge is also eliminated from his mind. Without the ability to know and the assurance of the validity of what he knows, man is helpless beyond imagination.

According to Scripture, when God created man, He gave to Adam two tasks which both required the development of knowledge. Adam was required to "dress" and "keep" the Garden of Eden (Gen. 2:15); i.e., to till it and to guard it. Man had to develop knowledge of horticulture and agronomy, and to realize that fruit trees and vegetables had to be protected from even unfallen animals if they were to produce. Again, Adam was required to name or classify the animals, a scientific task, so that again the development of knowledge was required (Gen. 2:19-20). Man's calling under God thus required the development of a body of knowledge. Because Adam was not then a fallen creature, it did not occur to him to doubt the validity of his sense impressions or to distrust whatever God said. The question, "Can we Know?," did not trouble him; he was too busy acquiring knowledge.

The tempter, however, raised an epistemological question, "Yea, hath God said, Ye shall not eat of every tree of the garden?" (Gen. 3:1). You have assumed, he declared, the validity of all your knowledge because you have assumed the absolute trustworthiness of God. How can you make so great an assumption? Your premise involves an unjustifiable act of faith. Declare your independence of God. Certainly, God is very powerful, and He perhaps can do what He chooses much of the time, but this is not *necessarily* so. "Ye shall not surely die" (Gen. 3:4). It is possible that you may, but that is not necessarily the case. By declaring your independence from God, you declare war on Him, and you risk reprisals. But, God's claims to the contrary, God has no eternal decree; there is no absolute predestination of all things by an absolute and sovereign God. You too have *being* as well as God. You can decree that tomorrow you will pick fruit, and it comes to pass. God does the same: He brings a greater and a senior power to bear on His determination of things, but it is not a *necessary* and *absolute* determination. God knows this and wilfully prevents you from having a true knowledge of your situation, and with good reason: "For God doth know that in the day ye eat thereof, then your eyes shall be opened, and ye shall be as gods, knowing good and evil" (Gen. 3:5). Every man can be his own god, knowing or determining for himself what constitutes good and evil. To know good and evil "signifies the right or authority to exercise independent discrimination between right and wrong." This means that "man was induced to take divine prerogatives in his own hand and set his own moral order."[2] Having done this, man thus sought to know all

---

[2.] Lester J. Kuyper, "To Know Good and Evil," in *Interpretation, A Journal of Bible and Theology* I, 4 (October 1947), 492.

reality apart from God. If God's interpretation of good and evil is false and is grounded on a desire to prevent man from knowing the truth, then God's interpretation of all reality is equally untrustworthy. *Facts*, instead of having been created, determined, and constantly governed by God, are then simply facts which equally confront God and man. God's superior ability to govern facts does not mean that man cannot govern them also.

Man therefore, in his ostensible autonomy which he seeks by his declaration of independence from God, has a problem of knowledge. He cannot accept God's word about the world or anything. Indeed, in time he distrusts every bit of knowledge which points to God, and calls the very existence of God into question. If God's interpretation of facts is biased and untrustworthy, then the very facts which point to God are equally to be distrusted. God may be no more than a wish-fulfillment, or a projection of our own nature onto the universe. The ground must be cleared of all myths and suppositions so that man can face the *facts* squarely and freely, without any misconceptions or predetermined patterns derived from religion.

Science is knowledge, and man must approach facts scientifically. He must also analyze the question of knowledge philosophically rather than religiously. *Epistemology* is the theory of knowledge. It comes from the Greek *episteme*, knowledge, and *logos*, word or theory. The basic question of epistemology is this: is knowledge possible? Man is inclined to answer dogmatically, "I know what I know." The philosophical skeptic is ready to agree, adding, "All you know is yourself, the *I*, so that, when you say, I know what I know, you know that you have ideas and sense impressions, and you are aware of the content of your mind. How do you know anything more than that?" The threat thus is solipsism (Latin: *solus*, alone, and *ipse*, self), that all you can know is yourself, so that the whole of reality, the external world and other persons, are simply representations of the self and have no independent existence. Modern philosophy, from Descartes to the present, is faced with this egocentric predicament. Man, having made himself his own ultimate and his starting point, is unable to know anything except himself. Having dispensed with God, man has also in effect dispensed with a knowable universe. As he tries to gain knowledge, he must know things in terms of himself. Are facts meaningful and verifiable in terms of man's experience and by man? The answer to this question has become a progressively instrumental and pragmatic answer. In other words, out of exhaustion over the philosophical impasse, philosophy has turned to a purely pragmatic approach: truth is what works; knowledge is that which gives me an instrument for the control of reality.

The problem of knowledge for modern unbelieving man is also complicated by his changing conception of himself. When man began his philosophical course of independence in Descartes, such a declaration of autonomy from God was not new. Greek philosophy had made it its starting point. Scholastic philosophy, by using Aristotle, had incorporated a large measure of the same autonomy into its system. Van Til has aptly observed, with respect to the difference this made to Scholasticism:

> It is natural, then, to ask how this difference between the Romanist and the Protestant concept of God should necessitate a specifically Protestant defense of Christianity as a whole. The reply would be as follows. The Protestant doctrine of God requires that it be made foundational to everything else as a principle of explanation. If God is self-sufficient then he alone is self-explanatory. And if he alone is self-explanatory then he must be the final reference point in all human predication. He is then like the sun from which all lights on earth derive their power of illumination. You do not use a candle in order to search for the sun. The very idea of a candle or of any other created light is that it is derivative. So the very idea of any fact in the universe is that it is a derivative. It cannot have come into existence by itself, or by chance. God himself is the source of all possibility.

On the other hand, if God is not self-sufficient and self-explanatory then he is no longer the final reference point in human predication. Then God and man become partners in an effort to explain a common environment. Facts then are not what they are in the last analysis by virtue of the plan of God; they are partly that, and they partly exist in their own power. And most basically of all, then, the human mind need not subject itself to the revelation of God as absolutely authoritative for him. He may defer to God as to an expert who has had greater experience than himself; but he need not make all thoughts captive to the obedience of Christ.[3]

Van Til points out that Arminianism, which has captured most of Protestantism, is based on the same premise as Scholasticism, and is an adaptation of it.

Modern man, however, no longer sees himself with the same confidence as he did in Descartes' day. His sin is no less great, but his self-evaluation has changed markedly. Man is no longer *res cogitens*, pure thinking substance, whose bodily passions are secondary to his sovereign intellect, but is now an animal whose being is governed by unconscious animal drives. Levi's comment is very much to the point:

The dominant critical problem of the twentieth century is to reconcile the role of the irrational in human conduct with the demand for reason in the ordering of society. The central position of this problem in our age derives from the intellectual history of the last three centuries of the West. It is, I think, the inevitable consequence of the conflict of two ideas, one the culmination of the intellectual climate of opinion of the seventeenth and eighteenth centuries, the other the outgrowth of the science of the nineteenth. It represents the confusion which inevitably results when the picture of the human individual implied in the philosophy of Rene Descartes is confronted with the picture of the human individual sketched in the biological science of Charles Darwin— when the picture of man the universal mathematician is

---

3. Cornelius Van Til, *A Christian Theory of Knowledge* (Philadelphia: Westminster Theological Seminary, 1954), 2; (Philadelphia: Presbyterian and Reformed Publishing Co., 1969), 12.

set side by side with the picture of man the well-trained animal. If an age takes both pictures seriously as the twentieth century has, it can hardly escape schizophrenia.[4]

Levi is right. Modern man's predicament leaves him tortured and schizophrenic. To deny that he is created in the image of God, modern man affirms that he has developed in the image of animals. To eliminate God, man has depreciated himself. To the modern avant-garde dramatist, the German, Max Frisch, "man cannot be free," or, if he tries freedom, "he finds that freedom is no better than bondage."[5] Jacques Audiberti regards all men as evil to begin with, and the sin of religion is that it makes men more evil.[6] Eugene Ionesco, in *The Chairs* (1952), held that communication between human beings is impossible, and there is no solution to the problem of man because there is no meaning.

> Life, Ionesco is saying, is a hell in which each person is imprisoned in his own separate soundproof cubicle, invisible and inaudible to everyone else. All so-called communication is illusory: the only person we really communicate with all the time is ourself.[7]

Most modern men have never heard of the existence of Descartes, Locke, Berkeley, Hume, and Kant, but the problems of knowledge raised by these men underlie the isolation and self-torment of modern man. Epistemology is an abstract and technical subject, but its consequences are intensely relevant to our everyday life. A study of epistemology thus brings us into the center of the modern dilemma.

[4.] Albert William Levi, *Philosophy and the Modern World* (Bloomington: Indiana University Press, 1959), 32.
[5.] George Wellwarth, *The Theater of Protest and Paradox* (New York: New York University Press [1964] 1967), 167.
[6.] *Ibid.*, 75.
[7.] *Ibid.*, 59.

2

Circular Reasoning

To keep too close an eye on philosophy is sometimes to neglect to note how closely it is related to life. Before examining the philosophy of factuality, let us see how a prominent writer of the 20th century viewed the predicament of man and of man's efforts to know. Albert Camus (1913-1960) saw man in revolt gaining nothing out of his revolt except unlimited slavery. It can be held that there are "only two possible worlds" conceivable to the thinking man, the world of grace and the world of rebellion. "The disappearance of the one is equivalent to the appearance of the other." Rebellion is now basic to modern man. "Unless we choose to ignore reality, we must find our values in it. Is it possible to find a rule of conduct outside the realm of religion and its absolute values? That is the question raised by rebellion."[1] Modern man, isolated by his epistemology, finds his solidarity only in rebellion. Whereas for Descartes, the starting point was, "I think, therefore I am," for man today "the first piece of evidence" is, "I rebel — therefore we exist."[2]

[1] Albert Camus, *The Rebel* (New York: Vintage Books, 1956), 21.
[2] *Ibid.*, 22.

The Marquis de Sade is a classic example of the modern rebel. For him all crimes are a virtue; all things are permitted, and all sexual perversions must be practiced with zeal as part of man's rebellion against God. "Since God claims all that is good in man, it is necessary to deride what is good and choose what is evil."[3] The rebel thus has a will to evil. He systematically rejects salvation. The rejection of God leads to the rejection of all things. Dostoyevsky's Ivan Karamazov declares, "It is not God whom I reject; it is creation."[4] Nietzsche held that this rejection required the rejection, of course, of God's law. He declared, "The advantage of our times: nothing is true, everything is permitted."[5] This, however, imposed a fearful burden on him:

> From the moment that man believes neither in God nor in immortal life, he becomes "responsible for everything alive, for everything that, born of suffering, is condemned to suffer from life." It is he, and he alone, who must discover law and order. Then the time of exile begins, the endless search for justification, the aimless nostalgia, "the most painful, the most heartbreaking question, that of the heart which asks itself: where can I feel at home?"[6]

Of the rebel, Camus observed, "Once he had escaped from God's prison, his first care was to construct the prison of history and of reason."[7]

For Camus, "the meaning of life is the most urgent of questions. How to answer it?"[8] Man has a "nostalgia for unity," an "appetite for the absolute." "The mind's deepest desire" is for clarity, familiarity, and understanding. "Understanding the world for a man is reducing it to the human, stamping it with his seal."[9] This is a logical conclusion for an existentialist like Camus. If the world is not God's creation, it must somehow be made man's creation. Sartre

---

[3.] *Ibid.*, 47.
[4.] *Ibid.*, 59.
[5.] *Ibid.*, 67.
[6.] *Ibid.*, 70.
[7.] *Ibid.*, 80.
[8.] Albert Camus, *The Myth of Sisyphus and Other Essays* (New York: Knopf, 1958), 4.
[9.] *Ibid.*, 17.

holds that man has being but no essence, no pre-ordained pattern or meaning. Man makes his own essence and pattern and defines himself. It follows that man also wants to remake the world in his own image.

Modern man feels an intense anguish as he confronts "a world I never made." Man wants the pattern of his imagination to govern reality, and, like God to utter the fiat word and to see reality born at the word of his mouth. The agony of the modern intellectuals is over the gap between their imagination and reality.

> With the exception of professional rationalists, today people despair of true knowledge. If the only significant history of human thought were to be written, it would have to be the history of its successive regrets and its impotences.
>
> Of whom and of what indeed can I say: "I know that!" This heart within me I can feel, and judge that it exists. There ends all I can touch, and I likewise judge that it exists. There ends all my knowledge, and the rest is construction.... This very heart which is mine will forever remain undefinable to me.[10]

We live in an absurd, meaningless world. Man is surrounded by "a horde of irrationals." "This world in itself is not reasonable, that is all that can be said. But what is absurd is the confrontation of this irrational and the wild longing for clarity whose call echoes in the human heart. The absurd depends as much on man as on the world." One rational fact could save the world: it would indicate that not all is contradiction and nonsense.

> The world itself, whose single meaning I do not understand, is but a vast irrational. If one could only say just once: "This is clear," all would be saved.[11]

---

10. *Ibid.*, 18f.
11. *Ibid.*, 27.

There is a conflict between man's existential "awareness" of the lack of essence, meaning, or pattern in the world, and man's urge for meaning:

> I can negate everything of that part of me that lives on vague nostalgias, except this desire for unity, this longing to solve, this need for clarity and cohesion. I can refute everything in this world surrounding me that offends or enraptures me, except this chaos, this sovereign chance and this divine equivalence which springs from anarchy. I don't know whether this world has a meaning that transcends it. But I know that I do not know that meaning and that it is impossible for me just now to know it. What can a meaning outside my condition mean to me? I can understand only in human terms. What I touch, what resists me — that is what I understand. And these two certainties — my appetite for the absolute and for unity and the impossibility of reducing this world to a rational and reasonable principle — I also know that I cannot reconcile them. What other truth can I admit without lying, without bringing in a hope I lack and which means nothing within the limits of my condition?[12]

Camus was paralyzed by his modern premises, his existentialism aggravating his condition. As a child of Descartes, he declared that "To think is first of all to create a world (or to limit one's own world, which comes to the same thing)."[13]

But Camus was right: modern philosophy cannot answer the basic question, "can we know anything?," affirmatively. Not at all surprisingly, philosophers in the modern tradition deny the historic function of philosophy. In particular, the philosophers in the logicoanalytic school (Moore, Wittgenstein, and Carnap) abandon the historical functions of philosophy as of no concern to them.

Some philosophers, such as Henri Bergson and Alfred North Whitehead, have still sought to understand the world in terms of some central concept. The existentialists like Heidegger and

---

12. *Ibid.,* 51.
13. *Ibid.,* 99.

Sartre also belong to this tradition. These men attempt to find some kind of rationale for their human concerns in some aspect of man and his experience. These men do not solve the problem of epistemology, although they are aware of it.

A second group is made up of pragmatists like Charles Peirce, William James, and John Dewey. Like the first group, an intense social concern is often present. Its approach to the problem of knowledge is pragmatic: truth is instrumental; it is what works.

The third school has already been mentioned, the logico-analytic school, which is totally opposed to all that has traditionally been regarded as philosophy. The extent of this rejection is apparent in the following statements from Rudolf Carnap (b. 1891), a very prominent member of this school:

> Among the metaphysical doctrines that have no theoretical sense I have also mentioned *Positivism*, although the *Vienna Circle* is sometimes designated as Positivistic. It is doubtful whether this designation is quite suitable for us. In any case, we do not assert the thesis that only the Given is Real, which is one of the principal theses of traditional Positivism. The name Logical Positivism seems more suitable, but this also can be misunderstood. At any rate it is important to realize that our doctrine is a logical one and has nothing to do with metaphysical theses of the Reality or Unreality of anything whatever. What the character of a *logical* thesis is, will be made clear in the following chapters.[14]

> The meaning of our anti-metaphysical thesis may now be more clearly explained. This thesis asserts that metaphysical propositions — like lyrical verses — have only an expressive function, but no representational function. Metaphysical propositions are neither true nor false, because they assert nothing, they contain neither knowledge nor error, they lie completely outside the field of knowledge, of theory, outside the discussion of truth or falsehood. But they are, like laughing, lyrics, and music, expressive.[15]

[14.] Rudolf Carnap, from chapter I of *Philosophy and Logical Syntax* (1935), cited in Morton White, *The Age of Analysis* (New York: Mentor Books, 1955), 216.
[15.] *Ibid.*, 219f.

The function of propositions is to be logical in terms of the only reality man knows, his mind, and not to aim beyond that. Propositions make sense only in this respect, it is held. There are no meanings beyond the words used in a proposition or beyond the people who use them. Wittgenstein's statement, "The meaning is the use," summed up his position and also made evident a kinship to John Dewey.[16]

Philosophy is thus closely linked to the realities of our time. What begins as a philosopher's idea can end in marching feet and bloody conquest. At the beginning of the modern era, men held that *knowledge is power*, and both science and philosophy began an eager quest for power through knowledge. As men despaired of the possibility of knowledge, they turned their attention to power. Rousseau developed the concept of the general will, Hegel the idea of the state as the incarnation of soul, mind, or spirit, and men like Dewey and Wittgenstein a pragmatic concept of truth and knowledge. "The meaning is the use." By the 1960s students were burning and destroying their universities, and their faith now was less in knowledge than in direct actions, or power. George Orwell had earlier declared, "If you want a picture of the future, imagine a boot stamping on a human face — forever."[17] The quest for knowledge had given way to the quest for power.

At the same time, faith rests now, not in God, in any Christian sense, nor in knowledge, as in the older humanism, but in *experience*, in the newer and pragmatic humanism. John Dewey, in 1930, wrote that:

> Faith was once almost universally thought to be acceptance of a definite body of intellectual propositions, acceptance being based upon authority — preferably that of a revelation from on high. It meant adherence to a creed consisting of set articles. Such creeds are recited daily in our churches. Of late there has developed another conception of faith. This is suggested by the words of an American thinker: "Faith is tendency toward action."

---

[16] *Ibid.*, 228.
[17] George Orwell, *1984* (New York: Signet Books, 1951), 203.

According to such a view, faith is the matrix of formulated creeds and the inspiration of endeavor. Change from the one conception of faith to the other is indicative of a profound alteration. Adherence to any body of doctrines and dogmas based upon a specific authority signifies distrust in the power of experience to provide, in its own ongoing movement, the needed principles of belief and action. Faith in its newer sense signifies that *experience itself is the sole ultimate authority.*"[18]

Dewey then added that "The greatest obstacle that exists to the apprehension and actualization of the possibilities of experience is found in our economic regime."[19] Let us examine Dewey's statement a little more closely. The older humanistic belief in the possibility of certain knowledge has given way to skepticism. The answer now is faith, but definitely not faith in the supernatural and triune God and His revealed word. Faith for Dewey means no body of intellectual propositions summed up in a creed but faith in experience. Whereas for the Christian faith is in God and His infallible word, for Dewey it is in experience, which has "the sole ultimate authority." Experience is thus beyond criticism, except perhaps by experience. "The possibilities of experience" can be actualized only in a new economic order, in the socialism of the Great Community. How do we know that this is so? We know that this is so because by definition for Dewey the new infallible word is experience.

He prefers experience because it is a "democratic and humane arrangement." Democracy promotes better human experience and human experience promotes democracy.[20] But how can we discriminate among experiences? The valid experience is the experience which promotes continuing growth and interaction. Growth towards what? Democracy, of course.[21] Dewey has argued from a *faith* in democracy and

---

[18.] John Dewey, in Albert Einstein, *et. al., Living Philosophies* (New York: World Publishing Company, [1930] 1941), 21. (italics added).
[19.] *Ibid.,* 30.
[20.] Joseph Ratner, ed., *Intelligence in the Modern World, John Dewey's Philosophy* (New York: Modern Library, 1939), 663.
[21.] *Ibid.,* 664f.

experience to prove that democracy and experience are good. All his conclusions are involved in and are aspects of his presuppositions. To his partisans, it is a marvellous exercise of "intelligence in the modern world." To an outsider, it is the dogmatism of a humanistic faith reciting its credo, and proving all things by reference to its articles of faith.

Circular reasoning is in fact unavoidable. All reasoning is circular reasoning; it begins with certain premises, and those premises contain within them the totality of possibilities for that faith. The Christian reasons from God to God-given, God-created and interpreted facts, whereas the humanist reasons from man to man-made interpretations of brute factuality. All reasoning is presuppositional, and on the systematic application of humanistic premises man can have no knowledge at all. The unbeliever gains his knowledge by borrowing Christian theistic premises while denying the God thereof. As Van Til has so well summed it up,

> The only alternative to "circular reasoning" as engaged in by Christians, no matter on what point they speak, is that of reasoning on the basis of isolated facts and isolated minds, with the result that there is no possibility of reasoning at all. Unless as sinners we have an absolutely inspired Bible, we have no absolute God interpreting reality for us, and unless we have an absolute God interpreting reality for us, there is no true interpretation at all.

> This is not to deny that there is a true interpretation up to a point by those who do not self-consciously build upon the self-conscious God of Scripture as their ultimate reference point. Non-believers often speak the truth in spite of themselves. But we are not now concerned with what men do in spite of themselves. We are concerned to indicate that the absolute distinction between true and false must be maintained when self-consciously adopted non-theistic and a self-consciously adopted theistic point of view confront one another.[22]

---

22. Cornelius Van Til, *An Introduction to Systematic Theology* (Philadelphia: Westminster Theological Seminary, 1951), 152f; 1971 ed., 147f.

For Dewey, all difference, contradictions, and problems are resolved by his ideal society, so that conflict is replaced by community.[23] Community is the unity of experience.

For Dewey, what Descartes demonstrated in its earliest form, and Kant made clear, was that the idea of knowledge meant essentially experience. What Kant called the synthetic unity of Apperception, or self-consciousness, is "the highest condition of experience, and in the developed notion of self-consciousness we find the criterion of truth. The theory of self-consciousness is method." Dewey continued:

> But this abstract statement must be further developed. It comes to saying, on the one hand, that the criterion of the categories is possible experience, and on the other, that the criterion of possible experience is the categories and their supreme condition. This is evidently a circle, yet a circle which, Kant would say, exists in the case itself, which expresses the very nature of knowledge. It but states that in knowledge there is naught but knowledge which knows or is known — the only judge of knowledge, of experience, is experience itself. And experience is a system, a real whole made up of real parts. It as a whole is necessarily implied in every fact of experience, while it is constituted in and through these facts. In other terms, the relation of categories to experience is the relation of members of an organism to a whole. The criterion of knowledge is neither anything outside of knowledge, nor a particular conception within the sphere of knowledge which is not subject to the system as a whole; it is just this system which is constituted, so far as its form is concerned, by the categories.[24]

If we had written this statement for Dewey, we would have been accused of caricaturing him. What Dewey said is, very simply stated, that his is indeed thinking in a circle; his is admittedly circular reasoning, but it is one "which expresses the very nature of knowledge!" Dewey has his own concept of infallibility, and, no less than with any Christian, he begins

---

[23.] Ratner, *op. cit.*, p. 435ff.

[24.] Joseph Ratner, ed., *John Dewey's Philosophy, Psychology, and Social Practice* (New York: G. P. Putnam's Sons, 1963), 39f.

with an act of faith. All he is saying in effect is that *his* act of
faith is by definition the true one, and that of the Christian is
by definition false.

The Christian theist self-consciously admits that his is an act
of faith, that his presupposition is the sovereign and triune
God of Scripture and His infallible word. As against the
unbeliever, he contends that the presuppositions of the
unbeliever, if logically adhered to, make knowledge
impossible, whereas the presuppositions of the Christian
undergird all knowledge. The negative apologetics developed
by Van Til undercuts all the claims of the unbeliever by
showing him that his knowledge is gained on borrowed
premises. Inconsistent Christianity, such as Arminianism,
incorporates into its system a rejection of the plan or decree of
God as all-inclusive and totally determinative of all reality.
Man is allowed a measure of independence from God. As Van
Til so plainly stated the case,

> Thus we are back at that arch foe of Christianity, namely,
> the idea of human ultimacy or autonomy. This idea of
> autonomy expresses itself in modern times by holding that
> in all that comes to man he gives as well as takes. Modern
> philosophy has, particularly since the day of Kant, boldly
> asserted that only that is real for man which he has, in part
> at least, constructed for himself.

> Nor is this modern form of manifestation of the would-be-
> autonomous man illogical. In every non-Christian concept
> of reality brute facts or chance plays a basic role. This is so
> because any one who does not hold to God's counsel as
> being man's ultimate environment, has no alternative but
> to assume or assert that chance is ultimate. Chance is
> simply the metaphysical correlative of the idea of the
> autonomous man. The autonomous man will not allow
> that reality is already structural in nature by virtue of the
> structural activity of God's eternal plan. But if reality is
> non-structural in nature then man is the one who for the
> first time, and therefore in an absolutely original fashion,
> is supposed to bring structure into reality. But such a
> structure can be only "for him." For, in the nature of the
> case, man cannot himself as a finite and therefore

temporally conditioned being, control the whole of reality. But all this amounts only to saying that modern philosophy is quite consistent with its own principles when it contends that in all that man knows he gives as well as takes. It is merely the non-rational that is given to him; he himself rationalizes it for the first time. And so that which appears to him as rationally related reality is so related primarily because he himself has rationalized it.

The modern form of autonomy expresses itself then both in a negative and a positive fashion. Negatively it assumes or asserts that which is "out there," that is, that which has not yet come into contact with the human mind, is wholly non-structural or non-rational in character.[25]

Although man knows little of the world "out there," as a matter of faith or presupposition the natural man assumes that it is unstructured and irrational. the positive aspect of his claim to autonomy is to declare that the world "out there" is workable only if man's mind or experience gives it a pattern. Kuhn, as a scientist, uses the concept of paradigms as a constitutive of science. He admits to circular reasoning; all proof originates with the scientific presupposition or paradigm. But what is the relationship of the "facts" of science to the "real" world?

But is sensory experience fixed and neutral? Are theories simply man-made interpretations of given data? The epistemological viewpoint that has most often guided Western philosophy for three centuries dictates an immediate and unequivocal, Yes! In the absence of derived alternatives, I find it impossible to relinquish entirely that viewpoint. Yet it no longer functions effectively, and the attempts to make it do so through the introduction of a neutral language of observations now seem to me hopeless.[26]

---

[25] Cornelius Van Til, *The Defense of the Faith* (Philadelphia: Presbyterian and Reformed Publishing Co., 1955), 157f.; 1967 ed., 140f.

[26] Thomas S. Kuhn, *The Structure of Scientific Revolutions* (Chicago: University of Chicago Press, Phoenix Books, 1964), 125. Also issued as Vol. II, No. 2, of the *International Encyclopedia of Unified Science* (University of Chicago Press, 1962).

Kuhn wants a real world such as Christians hold man has; he at one point speaks of paradigms as not only "constitutive of science" but also that there is "a sense in which they are constitutive of nature as well."[27] This implies that there is an ultimate decree of God in all of nature, but Kuhn will not consider this. He wants to use this possibility without admitting its reality and its logical conclusion, God and His eternal decree. He thus slips into his circular reasoning enough of God's order to keep science functioning. He admits that *purpose* and *law* in nature would cause "a number of vexing problems" to "vanish."[28] Kuhn actually operates in terms of *two* mutually exclusive paradigms or presuppositions. *First*, he begins with the autonomous mind of man as the lone source of law and meaning in a meaningless world. *Second*, he assumes at critical points that a real world of a meaningful nature, undergirded by God's law and decree, is the object of scientific inquiry rather than brute, meaningless, and utterly fortuitous factuality.[29]

Circular reasoning marks the thinking of men on all sides. The thinking of the unbeliever, however, involves a serious inconsistency: he introduces into his system ideas borrowed from Christian theism while denying its premises. On his own premises, as we shall see, he can know nothing.

---

27. *Ibid.*, 109.
28. *Ibid.*, 169f.
29. See R. J. Rushdoony, *The Mythology of Science* (Nutley, N. J.: The Craig Press, 1967), 85-91.

3

Facts and Presuppositions

Whitehead, in commenting on philosophic method, wrote,

> So far as concerns methodology, the general issue of the
> discussion will be that theory dictates method, and that
> any particular method is only applicable to theories of one
> correlate species. An analogous conclusion holds for the
> technical terms. This close relation of theory to method
> partly arises from the fact that the relevance of evidence
> depends on the theory which is dominating the discussion.
> This fact is the reason why dominant theories are also
> termed "working hypotheses."[1]

We can agree that "theory dictates methods" and that "the
relevance of evidence depends on the theory that is dominating
the discussion." This is another way of saying that
presuppositions determine or dictate what the facts shall be.

Whitehead, in order to preserve knowledge as a possibility,
broke to a degree with other philosophers to view the world as
an experienced process rather than atomistic particular
sensations. In this experienced process, Whitehead sought to
know brute facts and discern in them a pattern of endurance in

---

[1.] Alfred North Whitehead, *Adventures of Ideas* (New York: Mentor Books, 1955),
221.

process whereby some kind of knowledge would be possible. In effect, he echoed platonic ideas and sought to locate in process and its formlessness some kind of form.[2]

The problem which confronts all non-Christian philosophies, and all ostensibly Christian philosophies which presuppose to any degree the autonomy of man and a world of brute factuality, is very simply this: How can brute facts ever be anything more than brute facts?

For a consistent and biblically governed faith, all the facts of nature and history are the creation of the triune God. The facts of nature and history are totally governed by the God who ordained them and created them and who, by His eternal decree and comprehensive counsel, absolutely undergirds their every detail. All facts are thus God-given facts. As Van Til stated it, "All that may be known by man is already known by God. And it is already known by God because it is controlled by God"[3] All knowledge therefore is of God-created and God-interpreted facts.

This is not idealism. Idealism seeks to locate the meaning of facts within creation itself and it presupposes that facts in themselves are both form or idea and matter. Thus, Cecil De Boer in 1953 charged Van Til with idealism because he insisted on the impossibility of knowledge if a philosopher were consistent to his presupposition of brute facts. According to De Boer,

> The new apologetics maintains that the unbelievers in rejecting supernatural revelation, rejects the "first Premise" of all true reasoning and cannot, therefore, hope to come to a true conclusion. He may be as logical in his argumentation as he pleases, but since he is simply out of touch with reality, his reasoning cannot but end in sheer illusion. Therefore, he cannot really be said to "know anything truly." In short, unless I "know God truly," I cannot know anything truly.[4]

[2.] A. W. Levi, *Philosophy and the Modern World*, 495ff.
[3.] Cornelius Van Til, *The Defense of the Faith*, 116.
[4.] Cecil De Boer, "The New Apologetics," in *The Calvin Forum* XIX, 1-2 (August-September, 1953), 4.

Anyway, it is evidently useless to argue that because a man does not accept the Christian religion he cannot *really* (i.e., ultimately, metaphysically) distinguish an egg from a cucumber. That kind of thing gets one nowhere, and there is no earthly use for it except, possibly, as an undergraduate exercise in making purely nominal and academic distinctions.[5]

De Boer's charges were obviously ridiculous: a consistent creationism is the antithesis of idealism. Moreover, De Boer clearly conceded that Van Til is right, that a man who does not reason on strictly Christian grounds can know nothing if he confines himself to his premises. This is a point of inestimable importance. To call it simply "an undergraduate exercise in making purely nominal and academic distinctions" is an amazing statement and a fine example of camel-swallowing (Matt. 23:24). The history of modern philosophy witnesses to the fact that, on the premise of the autonomy of man in a world of brute factuality, knowledge becomes a critical problem and, indeed, impossible. Philosophy is not a game nor an undergraduate exercise; when philosophy, in developing the implications of its premises, is unable to account for the reality of our everyday experience and common knowledge, we have every right to question the validity of those premises.

When we reject the God of Scripture and posit a universe of brute factuality, we do create for ourselves some very serious problems. The idea of brute factuality does eliminate the Creator God of Scripture, but it leaves us with a perhaps infinite number of brute facts, totally irrational and impervious to reason, having no pre-established pattern or meaning and being thus essentially isolated and autonomous facts. As an existentialist, autonomous man can deny that he has any essence, any God-given nature and determination; he may insist that he has being and must make or define his own essence. Then, however, all other men and all other facts in the universe are in the same status: they have no essence, no pre-established pattern, no meaning, and hence no definition. In

---

5. *Ibid.*, 6.

such a situation, nothing can be known if a man is faithful to his presuppositions.

The consistent Christian position must be a demand that men must be consistent to their basic starting-point, to their presupposition. Their implicit metaphysical and epistemological principles will, if systematically carried out, require the unbeliever to admit his impasse. The point of Van Til's negative apologetics is to push the unbeliever to a recognition of his premises and of their inability to furnish him with any valid knowledge. The Christian must especially challenge the idea of neutrality. "In spite of this claim to neutrality on the part of the non-Christian, the Reformed apologist must point out that *every* method, the supposedly neutral one no less than any other, presupposes either the truth or the falsity of Christian theism."[6]

Facts are what our presuppositions assume them to be. If our presupposition is consistently Christian, the facts we confront are God-created and are governed, like ourselves, by His predestinating counsel. If our presuppositions are grounded on autonomous man in a world of brute factuality, then the reference point in all thinking is that omnipresent brute factuality. It is our presupposition that makes facts intelligible and determines what a fact is. Before we approach a "fact," our presupposition has determined what constitutes a "fact," so that when we ask, what is a "fact"?, we can answer the question only by looking at our presupposition. As Van Til has pointed out, with reference to this question,

> The answer to this question cannot be finally settled by any direct discussion of "facts." It must, in the last analysis, be settled indirectly. The Christian apologist must place himself upon the position of his opponent, assuming the correctness of his method merely for argument's sake, in order to show him that on such a position the "facts" are not facts and the "laws" are not laws. He must also ask the non-Christian to place himself upon the Christian position for argument's sake in order that he may be

6. Cornelius Van Til, *The Defense of the Faith*, 117; 1967 ed., 100.

shown that only upon such a basis do "facts" and "laws" appear intelligible.

To admit one's own presuppositions and to point out the presuppositions of others is therefore to maintain that all reasoning is, in the nature of the case, *circular reasoning*. The starting point, the method, and the conclusion are always involved in one another.[7]

The unbeliever does have valid knowledge because he does not think consistently in terms of his premises. He assumes a uniformity and order in nature; he proceeds on the presupposition that reality is not total irrationality but does in fact have a pattern which is rational and comprehensible. As a result, he does gain knowledge by assuming that the world is what God made it to be, while at the same time denying God and creation. As Van Til notes, some object, saying, "Do you mean to assert that non-Christians do not discover truth by the methods they employ?" The answer is, as Van Til points out, "nothing so absurd as that. The implication of the method here advocated is simply that non-Christians are never able and therefore never do employ their own methods consistently."[8] The Christian does not attempt to prove that God exists but to demonstrate that, apart from the presupposition of God, no proof is possible. The starting point of thinking should not be man, as in Descartes and modern philosophy (*cogito ergo sum*), but God.

Without the presupposition of God, there is no ground for distinguishing between one particular and another, because there would be no premise beyond autonomous man and brute factuality to establish a principle of differentiation and a pattern of meaning. Van Til has very ably illustrated this fact:

> Over against this Christian theistic position, any non-Christian philosophy virtually denies the unity of truth. It may speak much of it and even seem to contend for it, as idealistic philosophers do, but in the last analysis non-Christian philosophy is atomistic. This follows from the

---

7. *Ibid.*, 117f; 1967 ed., 100f.
8. *Ibid.*, 120; 1967 ed., 103.

absolute separation between truth and reality that was
introduced when Adam and Eve fell away from God.
When Satan tempted Eve to eat of the forbidden fruit he
tried to persuade her that God's announcement of the
consequences of such an act would not come true. That
was tantamount to saying that no assertion in terms of a
rational scheme could predict the course of movement of
time-controlled reality. Reality, Satan practically urged
upon man, was to be conceived of as something that is not
under rational control. Every non-Christian philosophy
makes the assumption made by Adam and Eve and is
therefore irrationalistic. This irrationalism comes to most
consistent expression in various forms of empiricism and
pragmatism. In them predication is frankly conceived of
in atomistic terms.[9]

Thus, when man makes his reason an autonomous judge over
all things, he also withdraws rationality from the universe in
that it is no longer the handiwork of God and therefore open
to reason because the absolute rationality of God created and
governs it. Man then sees himself as pure reason and the
universe as pure brute factuality, irrational factuality. The
problem then from Kant through Whitehead is to assert *and*
establish some kind of valid correlativity between logic and
fact, between the mind of man and a meaningless sea of
factuality.

The refuge of many thinkers, Lenin included, has been to
confess the epistemological dilemma and take refuge in a
"naive realism." Lenin wrote, in *Materialism and Empirico-
Criticism: Critical Notes Concerning a Reactionary Philosophy*:

> The "naive realism" of any healthy person, who is not an
> inmate of an insane asylum or in the school of the idealist
> philosophers consists in this, that he believes reality, the
> environment and the things in it, to exist independently of
> his perception — independently of his conception of
> himself in particular, and of his fellow men in general....
> Our sensation, our consciousness is only a representation
> of the outer world. But it is obvious that although a
> representation cannot exist without someone for whom it

[9.] *Ibid.*, 135; 1967 ed., 118.

is a representation, the represented thing exists independently of the one for whom it is a representation. The "naive" belief of mankind is consciously taken by materialism as the basis of its theory of knowledge.[10]

Except for some idealists and Christian Scientists, Lenin has no one to disagree with him. What he is saying about "naive realism" is that the world we perceive is assumed to be a real world. This we will grant him readily, because the real issue is that "naive realism" is actually an act of faith. Rather than accept the God of Scripture, Lenin chose to accept a world whose existence, in terms of his epistemology, he could not prove. To that world he assigned the attributes of God, including an eternal decree, or predestination, calling it instead the determinism of dialectical materialism.

All the attributes of the mind of God Lenin ascribed to materialism and then found manifested in a historical process of which he was the voice! When we begin with God as the Creator and Governor of all things, we can account clearly and rationally for the world of "naive realism." Without that God, we begin and end in a contradictory faith and pile miracle upon miracle in a vain attempt to account for a reality known to the village idiot. As Van Til observes,

> ....it is impossible to reason on the basis of brute facts. Everyone who reasons about facts comes to those facts with a schematism into which he fits the facts. The real question is, therefore, into whose schematism the facts will fit. As between Christianity and its opponents the question is whether our claim that Christianity is the only schematism into which the facts will fit, is true or not. Christianity claims that unless we presuppose the existence of God, in whom, as the self-sufficient One, schematism and fact, fact and reason apart from and prior to the existence of the world, are coterminous, we face the utterly unintelligible "brute fact."[11]

[10.] Lenin, *Materialism*, 47; cited in Levi, *Philosophy and the Modern World*, 216.
[11.] Cornelius Van Til, *Christian Theistic Evidences* (Philadelphia: Westminster Theological Seminary, 1947), 39; 1961 ed., 40.

For the consistent Christian thinker, because God is the maker of all things and their governor in terms of His eternal decree, there are no brute facts for God. With respect to His own person, God is totally self-conscious, and potentiality and actuality are one in Him; there is no unconsciousness in God nor any hidden and undeveloped possibilities. With regard to creation, "God's interpretation logically precedes the denotation and the connotation of all facts of which it consists."[12] Instead of beginning with brute facts, we begin with the God who created all facts, and all facts are meaningful and open to reason. The Christian position makes science possible, because it establishes the validity of a total pattern in all factuality. The only true explanation of every fact is in God, and therefore to operate on borrowed premises, to assume a pattern while failing to acknowledge either the pattern or its source, is to be inconsistent. The necessary self-existence of God must be our starting-point. "Accordingly, the various hypotheses that are to be relevant to the explanation of phenomena must be consistent with this fundamental presupposition. *God is the presupposition of the relevancy of any hypothesis.*"[13]

Let us again cite Van Til, whose work in this area puts all Christian thinkers in debt to him:

> It is important that we see the exact point at issue here. The Christian position is certainly not opposed to experimentation and observation. As Christians we may make various hypotheses in explanation of certain phenomena. But these various hypotheses will always be, as far as we can tell, in accord with the presupposition of God as the ultimate explanation of all things. Our hypotheses will always be *subordinate* to the notion of God as the complete interpreter of all facts, and if we make our hypotheses about facts subordinate to this God, it follows that there are no brute facts to which we can appeal in corroboration of our hypotheses. *We appeal to facts but never to brute facts.* We appeal to *God-interpreted*

---

12. *Ibid.*, 56; 1961 ed., 55.
13. *Ibid.*, 63; 1961 ed., 61.

facts. And this is simply another way of saying that we try to discover whether our hypothesis is *really* in accord with God's interpretation of facts. The ultimate test for the relevancy of our hypotheses is therefore their correspondence with God's interpretation of facts. True human interpretation is implication into God's interpretation.

In contrast to this, the ordinary scientific method seeks to determine the relevancy of hypotheses by an appeal to brute facts. An ultimate chance is assumed as the matrix of facts. Then the chance collation of facts is taken as the rational tendency among these brute facts. And the relevancy of an hypothesis is determined by its correspondence to this "rational tendency" in things. Thus the circle is complete. We start with brute facts and we end with brute facts. We presuppose chance as God, and therefore conclude that the God of Christianity cannot exist.

It is impossible to overemphasize the importance for Christians of seeing the difference between their position and the current scientific method on the three points that we have now considered. A Christian cannot allow the legitimacy of the ideal of complete comprehension. That this ideal is made a limiting rather than a constitutive concept does not improve matters, but, if possible, makes them worse. It clearly implies that God as creative and constitutive of reality and of true human interpretation is, from the outset, excluded. It means the elevation of chance to the place of God. Secondly, Christians cannot consistently allow the theoretical relevancy of every sort of hypothesis. This too implies an elevation of chance to the place of God. In the third place, Christians cannot allow the appeal to brute facts as a test of the relevancy of hypotheses. Once more this implies the elevation of chance to the position of God.[14]

Modern science is built on borrowed capital. It began with Puritan and Reformed thinkers who made the tremendous growth of science possible by their assumption of the eternal and predestinating counsel of God undergirding all reality.

[14.] *Ibid.*, 64; 1961 ed., 62ff.

This faith is denied in theory by modern science and assumed in practice. For the Christian, the universe manifests purpose because God created it and has a purpose for the universe. "It follows also that every fact within the universe has a purpose, or function to fulfill. Even that which we think of as mechanical has a purpose. Mechanical laws are, from the ultimate point of view, completely teleological."[15]

Instead of a universe (or multiverse) of brute factuality, in which there is no valid ground for assuming any relationship between one fact and another fact, the Christian thinker who is consistent to the presupposition of the Creator God of Scripture has a universe of inter-related facts whose principle of interpretation is in the sovereign and triune God. To assume that a sea of brute facts can give us anything more than brute facts is to believe, to cite Van Til's delightful illustration, that "the addition of zeros will produce something more than zero."[16] But there are no brute facts. They do not exist, except in the imagination of fallen man. There are only God-created facts, and all factuality, to be logically and rationally known and to be amendable to scientific investigation, requires the presupposition of the God of Scripture.

---

[15] *Ibid.*, 104; 1961 ed., 99.
[16] *Ibid.*, 76; 1961 ed., 73.

4

Faith and Knowledge

It is obvious, from what we have thus far discussed, that every epistemological system not only has a metaphysical basis (i.e., a concept of being), but also rests on pre-theoretical faith with respect to ultimacy. This primacy of faith is not only stressed in Scripture but developed in some of the church fathers, notably Tertullian and Augustine. It is clearly set forth in St. Anselm (1033-1109), who was called the second Augustine.

In his *Proslogium*, Anselm dealt with the problem of knowledge, beginning with the knowledge of God. In a moving summation of his predicament as he tried to know God, Anselm wrote:

> Lord, if thou are not here, where shall I seek thee, being absent? But if thou art everywhere, why do I not see thee present? Truly thou dwellest in unapproachable light. But where is unapproachable light, or how shall I come to it? Or who shall lead me to that light and into it, that I may see thee in it? Again, by what marks, under what form, shall I see thee? I have never seen thee, O Lord, my God; I do not know thy form. What, O most high Lord, shall this man do, an exile far from thee? What shall thy servant do, anxious in his love of thee, and cast afar from thy face? He

pants to see thee, and thy face is too far from him. He longs
to come to thee, and thy dwelling place is inaccessible. He
is eager to find thee, and knows not thy place. He desires
to seek thee, and does not know thy face. Lord, thou art
my God, and thou art my Lord, and never have I seen thee.
It is thou that hast made me, and hast made me anew, and
hast bestowed upon me all the blessings I enjoy; and not
yet do I know thee. Finally, I was created to see thee, and
not yet have I done that for which I was made.[1]

Knowledge, all knowledge, beginning with the knowledge of
God, was of intense concern to Anselm, but every attempt of
his reason to penetrate unaided the curtain of being led only to
frustration and contradiction. Every attempt to understand the
nature and essence of being resulted instead in his inability to
account rationally for what he knew, to use Lenin's phrase, by
"naive realism." As a result, Anselm turned his back on the
attempt of reason to function autonomously and rejected that
principle of Hellenic philosophy which was to become the
cornerstone of Scholasticism, the attempt "to understand that
I may believe." Instead, Anselm declared,

I do not endeavour, O Lord, to penetrate thy sublimity,
for in no wise do I compare my understanding with that;
but I long to understand in some degree thy truth, which
my heart believes and loves. For I do not seek to
understand that I may believe, but I believe in order to
understand. For this also I believe, — that unless I believed,
I should not understand.[2]

David declares, "For with thee is the fountain of life: in thy
light shall we see light" (Ps. 36:9). As against this, the principle
of Hellenic philosophy was, in effect, "In our light we shall see
Thee, O God, if Thou dost exist."

Although after Abelard philosophy used Aristotle's
premises in an attempt to understand in order to believe, the
conflict between the two positions went back to the early

[1.] Anselm, "Proslogium," in Sidney Norton Deane, trans., *St. Anselm: Proslogium;
Monologium; An Appendix in Behalf of the Fool by Gaunilon, and Cur Deus Homo*
(Chicago: Open Court Publishing Co., 1935), 3f.
[2.] *Ibid.*, 6f.

church. The fathers of the early church too often brought their philosophic presuppositions into the faith and attempted to reason from pagan premises to a Christian faith. Justin Martyr (100-165) assumed the monistic premise of Greek philosophy of a common being, so that, although he worshipped the triune God of Scripture, he reasoned from the Greek concept of being. He identified the Logos or Reason of Socrates with Jesus Christ and assumed a common framework of reference.[3] According to St. John, Jesus Christ "was the true light, which lighteth every man, [that] was coming into the world" (John 1:9). The presupposition of Scripture, however, is, among other things, the Creator-creature distinction, whereas the premise of Socrates was the continuity of being. Justin Martyr, because of his alien presuppositions, identified Christ with the reason of autonomous man and declared,

> We have been taught that Christ is the first-born of God, and we have declared above that He is the Word of whom every race of men were partakers; and those who lived reasonably are Christians, even though they have been thought atheists; as, among the Greeks, Socrates and Heraclitus, and men like them; and among the barbarians, Abraham, and Ananias, and Azarias, and Misael, and Elias, and any others whose actions and names we now decline to recount, because we know it would be tedious. So that even they who lived before Christ, and lived without reason, were wicked and hostile to Christ, and slew those who lived reasonably.[4]

In this vein, the unspoken conclusion would be that the Greek philosophers were better Christians than the apostles! Justin indeed did cite the philosophers and Stoics as witnesses of the faith while never acknowledging Christ or knowing Him.[5] For the Greek tradition, salvation meant identification with reason, and, in the neoplatonic tradition, absorption into the eternal idea or reason. For the Bible, salvation is not the

[3.] Justin Martyr, "First Apology," ch. V, in *Ante-Nicene Christian Fathers* (Grand Rapids: Eerdmans, 1967), I, 164.
[4.] *Ibid.*, ch. XLVI, 178.
[5.] *Ibid.*, "The Second Apology," ch. VIII, 190.

transition from unreason to reason but from sin and the wrath of God to grace through the atoning work of Jesus Christ.

For these two sharply divergent philosophies there are differing views of knowledge. For one who has within himself the same Reason which is the property of whatever God may be, the only problem of knowledge then is to apply reason carefully and strictly to the alien material world. The world of matter, in terms of the Greek dialectical philosophy of form (idea) and matter gives us God and man on one side, as possessors of a common being and rationality, alike at work trying to make sense and purpose out of a material world of brute factuality. The ancient and modern problems of epistemology stem from this dialectical problem, with its continual threats of a collapse of the dialectic into a monism or a dualism.[6] The medieval form of the dialectic was nature and grace, and the modern, freedom and nature.

Windelband, in his *History of Philosophy*, as well as Van Til, has called attention to the progressive indifference of Hellenistic and Roman philosophy to metaphysics and epistemology. Despairing of any solution, philosophers turned to a pragmatic approach and sought instead "wisdom for the conduct of life." The result, however, was a general skepticism because of the failure of philosophy "to solve the basic problems of being and of knowledge." As Van Til comments, "The world of unversality which has been projected by them as a means with which to explain the world of particularity gradually disappeared from sight into an endless fog of being without quality. The God of Aristotle was the purest of forms, the end-result of pure negation."[7]

Justin Martyr, for example, instead of beginning with the totally self-conscious, self-sufficient, and self-defined God of Scripture, who declares Himself to be the principle of all definitions and the self-existent One (Exodus 3:14), begins with

---

[6.] See R. J. Rushdoony, *The One and the Many* (Nutley, N. J.: The Craig Press, 1971).

[7.] Cornelius Van Til, *Christianity in Conflict* (Philadelphia: Westminster Theological Seminary, 1962), Part I, 25f.

a nameless God who is being. "But to the Father of all, who is unbegotten, there is no name given. For by whatever name He be called, He has as His elder the person who gave Him the name."[8] This sounds close to the statement of Exodus 3:14, except that for Justin the contrast is not between the uncreated being of God and all created being, but between being and "not-beings." This is apparent in Justin's "Hortatory Address to the Greeks." He quoted with approval such writers as Pythagoras on the unity of being, and God as "the intelligence and animating soul of the universe, the movement of all orbits."[9] Justin did hold to the uniqueness of Scripture and the truth of revelation, but he also sought common ground with the world in terms of the categories of autonomous reason. Justin asserted the exclusive saving power of Christ but then universalized Christ as the principle of reason and virtue in all men and opened salvation, as he had knowledge, to all men apart from the historical Jesus and yet in the eternal Logos.

Conflict thus entered into the church at the very beginning. Two different sets of presuppositions were brought together in an untenable union. The polarization of these sharply divergent tendencies was thus unavoidable. In Anselm one tradition found expression, and in Aquinas the other. In the Reformation the two fell apart, but not sharply enough, in that in some circles elements of the Hellenic presuppositions continued in the camps of the reformers, found expression in Arminianism, Bishop Butler, and others. Philosophically, the two traditions came together as Roman Catholic Descartes and Protestant John Locke operated under the same premise of autonomous man.

The skepticism which overwhelmed Greece and Rome followed in the wake of the Scholastics, and is with us again in the post-Kantian world. Philosophy has turned to pragmatism and has surrendered its traditional and inherent concerns. It seeks to relate logic and reality and cannot account for the correspondence it finds.

[8.] Justin Martyr, "Second Apology," ch. VI, in *Ibid.*, 190.
[9.] "Justin's Hortatory Address to the Greeks," ch. XIX, in *Ibid.*, 281.

Thus, Einstein, in *Essays in Science*, thinking with the background of modern epistemology, declared, "Pure logical thinking cannot yield us any knowledge of the empirical world; all knowledge of reality starts from experience and ends with it. Propositions arrived at by purely logical means are completely empty as regards reality."[10] For him, moreover, since our experiences are so inextricably mixed or united with concepts, they are never simply experiences, but rather intellectual conventions when we know them, even to the concept of causality. Having said all this, Einstein added candidly that his assumptions involved an enigma:

> At this point an enigma presents itself which in all ages has agitated inquiring minds. How can it be that mathematics, being after all a product of human thought which is independent of experience, is so admirably appropriate to the objects of reality? Is human reason, then, without experience, merely by taking thought, able to fathom the properties of real things?[11]

Levi reports that when Reichenbach asked Einstein how he discovered the theory of relativity, Einstein replied that he arrived at his conclusions because of his strong conviction of the harmony of the universe.[12] Thus, for Einstein concepts were merely conventions unrelated to reality: this was his philosophical premise. His operational premise, which led to his theory of relativity, was based on a view of the universe which presupposes the eternal decree of God.

The unbeliever thus has a schizophrenic position: on the one hand, he insists that a fundamental premise of sound thinking is to posit either the non-existence of God, or at the least to treat it as an open question, but not a momentous one, because man can ostensibly operate successfully without God. On the other hand, in everyday living, in the laboratory, and in his "naive realism," man insists on operating in terms of a universe created by the predestinating God of Scripture, who from all

---

10. Albert Einstein, *Essays in Science*, 14, cited in Levi, *Philosophy and the Modern World*, 262f.
11. Einstein, *Sidelights of Relativity*, 27, cited by Levi, 262f.
12. Levi, 263.

eternity has freely and unchangeably ordained all things that come to pass, without violence to any creature, nor by removing or infringing on the liberty or contingency of second causes, but rather establishing them.[13]

The issue thus is *not* that Anselm begins with faith and Aristotle, Plato, Aquinas, Descartes, or Kant begin with reason. *Rather, on both sides, men begin with faith.* The Christian begins with faith in the sovereign and triune God of Scripture. This is his starting point and his presupposition. The Christian does not begin by proving the existence of God, because God is the only source of all creation, of all interpretation, proof, and understanding. If we do not begin with God, we cannot logically know anything or prove anything: we are trapped in the narrow confines of our mind, in a cave of shadows and perhaps phantasies. We believe in order that we may understand.

The non-believers in the God of Scripture, and the schizophrenic Christians, begin by presupposing the autonomy of man's reason into a position of ultimate authority and judgment over all things. To assume this is a great act of faith. The Christian is not hostile to reason as reason, but to Reason as god. The Christian does not believe in reason; he believes in God and he uses reason under God.

For the consistent Christian, the point of departure is the sovereign God of Scripture. For modern man, it is the autonomous mind of man and its epistemic properties. As a result, modern man is caught between the two contradictory worlds of the rational (his mind) and the irrational (the world of brute factuality). The one realm is ruled by logic, and the other by chance. The one moves towards seeing a pattern, law, or order in all reality, and the other by definition is lacking in all these things.

The consequence of this tension between man and the outer world has not only been skepticism in the Greco-Roman, late medieval, and modern eras, but a crumbling of the sense of

---

[13.] See Westminster Confession of Faith, chapter III.

reality in both worlds. Bergson, in trying to re-establish knowledge, also raised the question as to how knowledge of the *inner* self is possible. Man began with "I think, therefore I am," in Descartes, but in the world of Freud, the unity and integrity of the *I* has been shattered.

In Descartes, man became pure thinking substance. In Darwin, this pure thinking substance was demoted to an animal status. In Freud, this man was reduced to the unconscious, primordial and untamed *id*, his pleasure principle, restrained only by the death principle of the *ego* and *super-ego*. The *ego* as the reality principle must constantly check-rein the dream world and the ancient urges of the *id*.

Freud, beginning with the premises of modern man, brought them to a suicidal conclusion. He was both a culmination of the Enlightenment faith and also its grave-digger. The old trust in man, in man's reason, and in man's ability to be rational and objective, was shattered trenchantly by Freud. To speak of an epistemology of Freud is to abandon philosophy. Freud's man projects the primordial nightmares of his unconscious world onto the world around him, and his ratiocinations are a better index to pathology than to epistemology. Freudian man can in essence really only know his misery and his impotence.[14]

Earlier, of course, Darwin had pointed to the same unhappy skepticism concerning the possibility of knowledge. In a letter of July 3, 1811, to W. Graham, Charles Darwin wrote:

> Nevertheless you have expressed my inward conviction, though far more vividly and clearly than I could have done, that the Universe is not the result of chance. But then with me the horrid doubt always arises whether the convictions of man's mind, which has developed from the mind of the lower animals, are of any value or at all trustworthy. Would any one trust in the convictions of a monkey's mind, if there are any convictions in such a mind?[15]

[14.] See R. J. Rushdoony, *Freud* (Philadelphia: Presbyterian and Reformed Publishing Co., 1965).

[15.] Francis Darwin, ed., *The Life and Letters of Charles Darwin* (New York: Basic Books), 1959, I, 285.

Can we wonder that epistemology has been neglected?

Gunther Stent, a professor of molecular biology, foresees the end of science because the principles of differentiation and value are gone. In a world where knowledge is in doubt, and where the reality principle has eroded, man is left with either a lust for power or for pleasure, and both alike portend the death of civilization and man.[16]

The times require a Christian epistemology.

[16.] Gunther S. Stent, *The Coming of the Golden Age: A View of the End of Progress* (Garden City, N. Y.: The Natural History Press, 1969), 77ff., 84, 88ff., 110ff., 135ff.

5

Epistemological Man

According to Scripture, the tempter offered to mankind a new epistemology, a way of knowing divorced from God. *First,* the tempter denied the truth of God's word, "yea, hath God said...?" (Genesis 3:1). Truth was divorced from God and given a separate existence as something God (or man) might or might not say, but which is separate and distinct from God. Scripture declares of God, that "Thy word is truth" (John 17:17), and "Thy law is truth" (Psalm 119:142). When Nebuchadnezzar believed in God, he declared Him to be "the King of heaven, all whose works are truth, and his ways judgment (or justice)," Daniel 4:37. By separating God from truth, the tempter made God irrelevant to epistemology. God, like man, is in the position of seeking to know an alien world and to comprehend it by means of reason.

Second, the tempter denied the eternal decree of God. All things are not under the total control of a predestinating God. "Ye shall not surely die" (Genesis 3:4). God, because of His superior position of power, can no doubt take effective reprisals against you for your declaration of independence, but there is no certainty about His threats. No ultimate and primary control rests in God's hands. An essentially free and open world of factuality is the product of chance and amenable to control by God or man, and it is up to free and autonomous man to take control. Man *may* die, but there is no eternal decree of God to require it. Death as a consequence of sin is not a necessity, and death as an aspect of life is open to scientific conquest. Man by his reason, having freed himself from God, can take control and abolish in time all the detrimental factors in his environment. He can take a world of brute factuality and impose upon it his own decree of determination or predestination.

Third, by your declaration of independence from God, "ye shall be as gods (or, as God), knowing good and evil" (Genesis 3:5). As Kuyper pointed out, to know good and evil "signifies the right or authority to exercise independent discrimination between right and wrong." Man was "induced to take divine prerogatives in his own hand and set up his own moral order."[1] Since reality is neither God's creation nor determined by His decree, and since truth is not identical with God and His word, then man is free to impose upon a world of brute and meaningless factuality that order which most pleases him. Man thus determines what constitutes good and evil, truth and falsehood, and then imposes that concept on the world around him. Man's word concerning these things is as valid as God's word.

This is the meaning of the temptation and of original sin. Man has opposed to God's word his own word, and to God's law, the law of man's imagination. Man refuses to submit to anyone save himself or to know reality except in terms of his own fiat reason.

There are some churchmen who imagine that, if only we present the indubitable facts of the resurrection to unbelievers, we will clearly convince them of the truth of the gospel. They will, in effect, be saved by the conclusions of the same apostate reason which denies God and sets itself up as god!

[1.] Lester J. Kuyper, "To Know Good and Evil," in *Interpretation, A Journal of Bible and Theology*, I, 4 (October, 1947), 492.

Van Til, in a very telling pamphlet, *Paul at Athens*, deals precisely with this point. When Paul at Athens preached concerning the resurrection, he immediately attracted great interest from the philosophers. They were greatly interested in such a possibility, because from their perspective, the universe was not the determined work of the sovereign God but a product of chaos.

> They believed in "the mysterious universe"; they were perfectly willing therefore to leave open a place for "the unknown." But this "unknown" must be thought of as the utterly unknowable and indeterminate.[2]

An unknowable universe is one which thus has no pre-determined nature or meaning; it is open to the imperialism of man as the new god of being to impose thereon his own fiat word and thereby make it his own. The world therefore should be full of open possibilities, which man can develop and exploit, but no certainties which limit man to a pre-determined course and possibility. As Van Til analyzes the attitudes of the hearers of St. Paul,

> They were a bit suspicious, shall we say, because of what they had heard Paul say about Jesus and the resurrection in the market place. But he is no common revivalist; so let us hear him out. Let us take him away from the rabble and ask him to make clear to us what he means by Jesus and the resurrection. Maybe there are such things as resurrections. Aristotle has told us about monstrosities, has he not? Reality seems to have a measure of the accidental in it. And if anywhere, history is the realm where the accidental appears. So maybe he has something strange to tell us. We have an Odditorium in which there is some vacant place.[3]

In a word, the resurrection was to them a possibility if it appeared out of a world of chaos, as a new instance of possibility or *Potentiality*. The philosophers of Athens were ready to accept the resurrection as a historical fact in the same way they viewed the historical appearance of a two-headed calf.

[2.] Cornelius Van Til, *Paul at Athens* (Phillipsburg, N. J.: Grotenhuis, 1954), 6.
[3.] *Ibid.*, 7f.

The resurrection had to be forced into the Procrustean bed of their philosophy or else rejected.

St. Paul, however, set the resurrection of Jesus Christ in the context of the sovereign decree of God and the inescapable fact of God's judgment on sin. The reaction then was either to mock Paul or to brush him off with, "We will hear thee again of this matter" (Acts 17:32). St. Paul, by challenging their concept of the unknown god, and by asserting the sovereignty of the revealed God of Scripture (Acts 17:22-31), had challenged their entire philosophy. He had in effect declared, as Van Til points out,

> ...What is the relation between the gods you say you know and the god of gods you say you do not know? Is it not the same reality, the same universe of which in one breath you say that it is wholly unknown and also that it is wholly known? If there is that in the universe which, on your system, is wholly unknown, and if this which is wholly unknown has an influence for good or evil on that which you say you know, do you then really know anything at all? Why not destroy all the altars to the gods you say cannot be known? On your basis it is impossible to know anything unless you know everything, and since by admission you do not know everything you should admit that the whole of your religious activity is an irrational procedure. And what is true of your religion is true of your science. You do not know what water, earth, air and fire are. You appeal to some common principle above them all from which as a common source they spring. But then this common source, has, as Anaximander said, no positive quality at all. It must be without quality to be truly beyond and thus truly common, and when truly beyond and therefore without quality, it cannot serve as the explanation of anything that has quality in the world you claim to know.
>
> Your worship is therefore one of ignorance, of ignorance far deeper than you are willing and able on your assumption to own. On your basis there is no knowledge at all; there is nothing but ignorance.

But worse than that, your ignorance is not only much deeper than you own; it is of a wholly different character than you think it is. It is ethical, not metaphysical in character. You are making excuse for your ignorance on the ground that you are finite and that the world is infinite. And you make an altar to a god whom you speak of as unknown to man at all. He is not unknown to you.[4]

Autonomous man is aware of the deadly impasse that his epistemology leads him into. From ancient times he has been aware of the fact that the world of experience cannot be accounted for or trusted in terms of his premise of autonomy. The moral fact which governs the situation is that man prefers to be an idiot god to being a learned man under God. As a result, he clings to his epistemology for theoretical reasons while for practical purposes assuming that the world is undergirded by God and His sovereign decree.

As we saw earlier, the tempter insisted on separating truth and a knowledge of reality from God. It is not God and truth which are identical, but truth and knowledge are alike available to God and man on investigation. However, a truth and knowledge which are not of God are then possibly aspects of the being of brute factuality. We cannot know this for sure, since we have no exhaustive knowledge of that world of brute factuality. It can be that brute facts, as they evolved by chaos, have accidentally developed some kind of pattern or patterns. We may have a universe out there, or we may have a multiverse, a number of patterns. Again, we may have a vast number of brute facts which are each of them a pattern and universe unto themselves. Still further, every brute fact can be simply that and nothing more, without purpose, pattern, or meaning, and all meanings and laws can be made by man and purely conventional. Until we have an exhaustive knowledge of reality, we cannot say. This exhaustive knowledge will involve a total knowledge not only of all factuality in the universe at any given moment, but also of all history from the first atom's "birth" to the present. Since this is obviously

---

[4] *Ibid.*, 8f.

impossible, knowledge is obviously impossible also. If truth and knowledge can have no place in the factuality around us, then, having been detached from God, and from a platonic relationship to factuality, their locale is then obviously in man.

Instead of now declaring of God, "Thy word is truth" (John 17:17), we must then declare of man, "thy word is truth." Man's fiat word is truth, and it is knowledge. Man is now the new ultimate, and it is the word of man rather than the word of God by which all things must be judged. Thus, a young scientist, whose academic and research credentials were paltry when compared to those of a distinguished man of science who was a creationist, all the same asserted categorically of the creationist that his work was not "scientific." His reason was not a criticism of the experiments of the man but of his presuppositions: anyone who saw the word of God as authoritative as against the word of scientific man was by definition not a man of science, no matter what he might say or do. Man has made himself the ultimate point of reference and has specifically excluded God. This, of course, has a far-reaching implication for epistemology, as Van Til pointed out:

> For the question of knowledge this implied the rejection of God as able to identify himself in terms of himself and with it the rejection of God as the source of truth for man. Instead of seeking an analogical system of knowledge, man after this sought an original system of knowledge. And this meant that God was reduced with him to the necessity of seeking truth in an ultimately mysterious environment. In other words, it implied that in setting up himself as independent man was declaring that there was no one above him on whom he was dependent. But man even then knew that he was not ultimate. He knew that he had no control of reality and its possibilities. So what his declaration of independence amounted to was an attempt to bring God down with himself into an ocean of the irrational.

> This effect on knowledge, it may be indicated in passing, is equivalent to the effect of bringing God down into the realm of abstract possibility in the field of being. Abstract

possibility in metaphysics and ultimate mystery in epistemology are involved in one another. To this must be added that in ethics this involved the denial of God's right to issue any commandment for man.[5]

Man and God are alike afloat on a vast ocean of chance which is also shoreless and bottomless. Neither God nor man can know anything save that they are, in terms of this viewpoint. Man knows that he is, but not what he is; he has being, Sartre holds, but no essence. Man prefers this condition of radical ignorance to a condition which gives him knowledge under God.

The reason for man's willful choice of ignorance is not ignorance of the issues but sin. The epistemological problem has roots in a false metaphysics, but both alike stem from a moral choice, man's sinful desire to be his own god. In Darwin and Freud, man is reduced to the level of the animals. For Freud, the will to live in man is essentially his primordial urges to incest, parricide, and cannibalism, and the will to death is the ego's inhibiting reality principle which inhibits these three urges. The picture of man in Freud is clearly a very low one. More recently, Robert Ardrey has depicted man, not only as an animal, but as a beast of prey. Still other works, such as Colin M. Turnbull's *The Mountain People* (1972), give a still grimmer view of man. All of these studies, however, are beside the point. They judge man in terms of humanistic standards, and the sins of man are seen as a part of the process of development and self-realization. In reality, sin is man's rebellion against the law of God and man's attempt to be his own god, to replace God's word with man's word. Man the sinner denies that he is under the judgment of God and inescapably judged by the law of God.

Man seeks to escape from the law requirements of God and to establish his own law and to control the whole of reality by his fiat word. He therefore excludes the sovereignty of God and the authority of His law word, because man cannot allow

---

5. Cornelius Van Til, *A Christian Theory of Knowledge*, 30; 1969 ed., 47f.

such a God to exist in his world and to speak with authority to man. He will concede that such a God is possible, because, in terms of his view of reality, all things are possible. As Van Til observes,

> ...And thus it would seem that the existence of such a God as the Bible speaks of may also be possible. But when the natural man says that for him anything is possible and that therefore he has an open mind for the evidence of anything that may be presented to him, this assertion has a basic limitation. When he says that anything is possible, this is for him an abstraction or a limiting concept. He knows that cows cannot jump over the moon except in fairy tales. So the idea of a God whose experience is not subject to the same conditions as those that control man is not *practically* possible. Such an idea, he says, is meaningless. It is without intelligible content. It is the mere assertion of a *that* without an intelligible *what*. It is therefore pure irrationalism.
>
> On the other hand the Christian notion of Biblical authority is said to be pure rationalism. It would require a view of rationality as controlling whatsoever comes to pass. It would give man no measure of independence: his own reason would be of a piece with that which is predetermined from all eternity by God. Thus there would be no authority at all because authority implies the freedom of one person over against another.
>
> The non-Christian is quite consistent with his own principles when he thus rejects the Christian claim to authority as well as the Christian claim to the necessity of Scripture. How could there be any necessity for that which is inherently meaningless and outside the realm of practical possibility. How can we say that man has sinned against a God who exists in isolation from man and yet places irrationality upon him by making demands out of accord with the nature of human personality?[6]

The basic reality for modern epistemological man is his autonomous existence. This presupposition undergirds all his thinking and acting. It is the logical conclusion of life and

---

[6.] *Ibid.*, 38; 1969 ed., 58.

thought from the premise of Descartes. Thus, Arthur Schopenhauer (1788-1860), in the famous first paragraph of *The World as Will and Idea* (1819) made a logical conclusion:

"The world is my idea": this is a truth which holds good for everything that lives and knows, though man alone can bring it into reflective and abstract consciousness. If he really does this, he has attained to philosophical wisdom. It then becomes clear and certain to him what he knows is not a sun and an earth, but only an eye that sees a sun, a hand that feels an earth; that the world which surrounds him is there only as an idea, *i.e.*, only in relation to something else, the consciousness, which is himself. If any truth can be asserted *a priori*, it is this: for it is the expression of the most general form of all possible and thinkable experience: a form which is more general than time, or space, or causality, for they all presuppose it; and each of these...is valid only for a particular class of ideas; whereas the antithesis of object and subject is the common form of all these classes, is that form under which alone any idea of whatever kind it may be, abstract, or intuitive, pure or empirical, is possible and thinkable. No truth therefore is more certain, more independent of all others, and less in need of proof than this, that all that exists for knowledge, and therefore this whole world, is only object in relation to subject, perception of a perceiver, in a word, idea. This is obviously true of the past, and the future, as well as of the present, of what is farthest off, as of what is near; for it is true of time and space themselves, in which alone these distinctions arise. All that in any way belongs or can belong to the world is inevitably thus conditioned through the subject, and exists only for the subject. The world is idea....[7]

Schopenhauer, more ruthless than others, followed a course pursued by Oriental philosophy: he reduced the world to illusion, to an objectification of the will, insofar as reason is concerned. Only by intuition can man know the thing-in-itself. The thing-in-itself, however, is *will*, and reason is secondary to will. Will is the only reality, and differences are

---

[7.] Will Durant, ed., *The Works of Schopenhauer* (Garden city, N. Y.: Garden City Publishing Co., 1928), 3.

only illusions (or aspects of will). Schopenhauer held to a pantheism of the will; the world is a unity, but an idea, and as such an illusion.

> In this world of phenomena true loss is just as little possible as true gain. The will alone is; it is the thing-in-itself and the source of all these phenomena. Its self-knowledge and its assertion or denial, which is then decided upon, is the only event-in-itself.[8]

In the epistemology of modern man, the world as the creation of the sovereign God has given place first to the world as an aspect of man's experience and then to an illusion created by the will of man. Man, at the same time, has stopped regarding himself as the vice-gerent of God, created in His image, and has seen himself as a fragmented being ruled by ancient urges and lusts which control him and reduce his reason to a facade for rampant irrationalism. Not surprisingly, T. S. Eliot saw modern man as a shadow of man in a waste land of his own making.

---

8. *Ibid.*, 105.

6

Irrational Man

As we have noted, man, in the modern world view began by viewing himself, in Descartes, as a pure thinking substance, and he now regards himself at best as an irrational animal. The consequences of this are everywhere with us.

Van Til has commented, with respect to the Arminian view of the mind of man as independent from any ultimate decree of God, that

> Arminianism has been untrue to the Biblical point of view with respect to this matter. We usually think of Arminianism first of all with respect to its denial of the Biblical teaching of the sinner's inability. However, back of the error of Arminianism at this point lies the error to which we are now calling attention, namely, that it starts with the human consciousness as an ultimate instead of a derivative starting point. Arminianism has, in principle, denied the Biblical concept of creation. This is its basic error and the source of all its other errors. So, for instance, Professor Donald Mackenzie in his article on "Free Will" in the *Encyclopedia of Religion and Ethics* says that the trouble with Augustinianism and Calvinism is that it has started with the idea of an absolute God, and deduced the doctrine of decrees from it, while in reality we should start

from experience and adjust the concept of the absoluteness
of God's grace as best we can do it. It is this assumption of
human experience as an ultimate starting point that has
now led him into the further error of the acceptance of
modern irrationalism in the form of paradox theology.[1]

Having cut loose from God, and from the world as God's
creation, man now denies that philosophy can create or
maintain the possibility of a *system* of thought. Since no
pattern exists in the world of brute factuality, a system cannot
be derived from it, because a system implies an absolute decree
undergirding reality and giving it a pre-established pattern.

Thus, Dr. Joseph Haroutunian, in his inaugural address as
Cyrus H. McCormick Professor of Systematic Theology,
proceeded to deny the very idea of systematic theology. He
held that systematic theology forces reality on to a Procrustean
bed which disfigures and mutilates reality in order to compel
it to conform to a system.

> "Systematic theology" aping science has been dogmatic,
> for it has refused to subject the "essence of religion" to
> criticism. It has been speculative because its "rigorous
> deductions" have not been open to genuine verification.
> And when not sure of its own rationality, it has turned
> mystical or pragmatic, thus insuring itself against
> intellectual criticism. And it has also been irrelevant, for
> no system does itself justice to the complexities of human
> life. Existence is commerce with contingency, and ethical
> decision is a leap into the unknown. Hence the application
> of any system of theology to the infinite vicissitudes of life
> can only be partial and problematic. For these reasons,
> theology has earned a common reputation of pompous
> dullness.

> Now, I regret this as much as anyone here, and I promise
> you to do something about the matter. As a foretaste of my
> coming labors towards making the theology a more
> illuminating and therefore more interesting affair, I offer
> you the following reflections.

[1.] Cornelius Van Til, *An Introduction to Theology* (Philadelphia: Westminster Theological Seminary, 1947), I, 67.

The first step towards a non-boring theology consists in recognizing that "systematic theology" is an illusion.[2]

Scripture declares of the God of Scripture that "Known unto God are all his works from the beginning of the world" (Acts 15:18). St. Paul says of God's eternal decree,

> And we know that all things work together for good to them that love God, to them who are the called according to his purpose.
> For whom he did foreknow, he also did predestinate to be conformed to the image of his Son, that he might be the firstborn among many brethren.
> Moreover whom he did predestinate, them he also called: and whom he called, them he also justified: and whom he justified, them he also glorified. (Romans 8:28-30).

For such a God, predestination is an inescapable consequence of His sovereign power in creation. A system is thus also inescapable because God's eternal decree absolutely controls all things. To eliminate systematic theology requires eliminating such a God, or to retain Him only as a limiting concept. This Haroutunian does:

> "The Living God" of the Bible defies literal statement. It is analogical in so far as God must be conceived in the likeness of life as we know it. The Biblical man whose reflection concerned existence and destiny, and not "intellectual objects," spoke of the mysterious Intruder, fittingly, as the *"living God."* The living, powerful, encountering and acting God, who is responsive to man and to whom man is responsible, must be metaphorical: a carry-over, a projection from nature. God is not a thing among things, and does not live in the likeness of the creature. If God is living, according to all we know about life, He must have been born, and one day He will have to die. But the god of the Bible is eternal. Therefore He is living in a metaphorical sense. God is literally neither living nor non-living. "The living God" is thus a poetic expression. It is ambiguous, not in the sense of being vague or diffuse, but in that its signification is complex and

---

[2.] Joseph Haroutunian, *First Essay in Reflective Theology* (Chicago: McCormick Theological Seminary, 1943), 10.

inexhaustible. It is poetic, not in the sense of being
fanciful, but in that it is imaginative, evoking an image
which forbids identification with the Real. The Biblical
mind, which recognized God as the Creator of nature and
not a thing in it, and was free from the sophisticated
confusion between existence and "pure thought," filled its
discourses on God with images from nature, determined
not to identify God with anything in "heaven above or on
earth below or in the sea." The image both affirms and
denies its likeness to the Imagined. Therefore, Biblical
language is continually paradoxical. A paradox is a tension
between thesis and antithesis, an affirmation and a denial.
It is also two images in opposition, pointing to their
harmony in God: such as the loving God and the wrathful
God, which insist upon their reconciliation in the hidden
God. A paradox in the Bible is truth which can only be
perceived in the form of a contradiction bearing witness to
its own superficiality. Hence it constrains the mind to dig
into its meaning: with the promise of indefinite
penetration and clear warning that the quest is endless and
its goal beyond all intellection. Thus it is that the Bible
remains a source of illimitable insight into existence and a
whirlpool in which all systems are drawn into the mystery
of God.

Now, what happens when our science-possessed system-
making theologians set out to "translate" the language of
the Bible into another which shall be free from symbol
and metaphor, from the contamination of image and
emotion — precise, literal, and unparadoxical? If they
carry out the task they undertake (and we find our
theological scientists consistently refusing to do so), their
translations are in fact *mis*-translations. The "living God"
of the Bible becomes the first cause, or ultimate Being, or
a value producing factor in the universe, or the principle
of a living mind in its intercourse with God. But as
translations of "the living God," they are mis-
representations of Biblical religion. The notion of the first
cause has no context except if one smuggles some into it
from the paradox-ridden world of experience. "Ultimate
Being" is another paradoxical notion hovering between
the idea of a being, which turns God into an idol, and the

idea of "being in general," which is the undefinable least common denominator of all being.[3]

In this address we have the major currents of modern thought and modern theology very plainly set forth. Let us examine a few of the more relevant ones which are of concern to our interest. *First*, Haroutunian denies the validity of the term "the living God" except as a metaphor. For him, "God is literally neither living nor non-living." He also holds that, "If God is living, according to all that we know about life, He must have been born, and one day He will have to die." This is a most revelatory point. Clearly, Haroutunian did not look to Scripture for knowledge but to human experience exclusively, *i.e.*, "to all that we know about life." The meaning of *life* thus is understood in terms of man, not God. The limits of life are the limits of human experience. If man, who has life, dies, it follows that all life dies. This is *anthropomorphism* with a vengeance. Haroutunian has done more than renounce systematic theology: he has renounced theology in any form for anthropology. Man is his new creator, interpreting life in terms of the limits of his own life and experience. The humanistic scientist says, "What my net does not catch is not fish," and thus defines factuality only in terms of his pre-conceived limitations which are designed to eliminate God-created factuality. Haroutunian says that any life that transcends man's life and experience cannot be life. His idea of God "forbids identification with the Real," so that we do not have the living God of Scripture who performs great miracles and absolutely predestines and governs all things, but a limiting concept.

Second, Haroutunian insists that "the Biblical mind" was in some way "free from the unsophisticated confusion between existence and 'pure thought.'" This is an amazing statement. It reads back into the Bible the sophisticated distinctions and confusions of modern epistemology and then calls "the Biblical mind" an essentially post-Kantian mind. For Haroutunian

---

[3.] *Ibid.*, 12f.

existence means a world of meaningless brute factuality, and pure thought or reason has no relationship to such a world. Meaning and non-meaning cannot be confused. To think of God as "out there" is thus for him impossible. It ascribes meaning to a realm of non-meaning and projects as an entity into the outer world something which cannot be thought of as being, life, or substance. This is simply reading the Bible in terms of Immanuel Kant, and Haroutunian's "Biblical mind" is the mind of a devout disciple of Kant.

Third, he insisted that "Biblical language is continually paradoxical," *i.e.*, it is not an actual description of reality. It is imagery, and "The image both affirms and denies its likeness to the Imagined." "The Imagined" is a good name for the god of modern theology! Why is Biblical language always paradoxical? A paradox, he explained, is a tension between thesis and antithesis, between two images in opposition; it is an affirmation and a denial, "a contradiction bearing witness to its own superficiality." We are thus plainly in the world of dialectical theology. The Bible is not dialectical. Greek philosophy, Scholasticism, and modern philosophy are all dialectical. To project the problem of dialecticism onto the Bible is to refuse to take the Bible on its own claims and statements. It is an insistence that it can only be read with the mind of a post-Kantian man. Truth is beyond "all intellection" for such a mind, because the reality "out there" is beyond reason and meaning (as well as beyond life) and is therefore beyond truth, which is inseparable from reason and meaning. All we have is "the mystery of God" in a post-Kantian sense as that which is without meaning or pattern. Because this non-living God is beyond "intellection," beyond truth and meaning, very obviously this God is also beyond any possible system. Systematic theology is by definition an impossibility.

Fourth, since this God of dialecticism is beyond system and meaning, and beyond life, to speak of Him as "Ultimate Being" is to turn God into an idol, a fact or thing. To speak of God as the first cause (or any kind of cause) is to place Him in that outer world of brute factuality and to insist on a meaning governing that world. Haroutunian wants only a reflective theology which will use God as a limiting concept. Theology cannot be "scientific," *i.e.*, a form of knowledge or a body of knowledge, because we have no knowledge of God, no deposit of truth in Scripture that we can know as a true account of the real and living God. Theology must be divorced from science, which means that it must cease to be systematic, because the idea of a system requires a universe of total meaning governed by absolute rationality.

> Let us therefore call a halt to theology which is "hell bent" for "science" and the system. I deny that theology can be scientific, because God is not a thing among things. I deny that systematic theology is possible, because the paradoxes of the Christian faith signify the mystery of God who resists inclusion in any "system of nature." The time has come to do away with the error and arrogance of "scientific" theology and system-making, and to break the stranglehold of a theological method which has for too long devitalized the mind of the Church.[4]

Such a statement is a remarkable instance of the arrogance of modern irrational man, who has devitalized the church and blames the Christians for doing it! It is an irrational mind by its own willful desire. As Knight has observed, "The 'irrationality,' 'despair,' and so forth of modern thought reside precisely in its refusal to believe in the possibility of system."[5]

One consequence of this irrationality is the idea of the *absurd.* The source of the absurd is the contrast between the unintelligible, irrational, and meaningless nature of the world around us, and man's reason. Camus declared,

> I said that the world is absurd, but I was too hasty. This world in itself is not reasonable, that is all that can be said. But what is absurd is the confrontation of this irrational and the wild longing for clarity whose call echoes in the human heart. The absurd depends as much on man as on the world. For the moment it is all that links them

---

[4.] *Ibid.,* 20.
[5.] Everett W. Knight, *Literature Considered as Philosophy, The French Example* (New York: Collier Books, 1962), 17.

together. It binds them one to the other as only hatred can
weld two creatures together. This is all I can discern clearly
in this measureless universe where my adventure takes
place.[6]

An early forerunner of the idea of the absurd was Matthew
Arnold (1822-1888), who, in "Dover Beach," wrote of the
departure of meaning from the world as Christian faith waned.
As surely as a receding tide leaves a draining shore behind it, so
surely a waning Christian faith leaves behind it a world empty
of all truth and meaning. In the concluding section of "Dover
Beach," Arnold wrote:

> The Sea of Faith
> Was once, too, at the full, and round earth's shore
> Lay like the folds of a bright girdle furled.
> But now I only hear
> Its melancholy, long, withdrawing roar,
> Retreating, to the breath
> Of the night wind, down the vast edges near
> And naked shingles of the world.
> Ah, love, let us be true
> To one another! for the world, which seems
> To lie before us like a land of dreams,
> So various, so beautiful, so new,
> Hath really neither joy, nor love, nor light,
> Nor certitude, nor peace, nor help for pain;
> And we are here as on a darkling plain
> Swept with confused alarms of struggle and flight
> Where ignorant armies clash by night.

With Arnold, Camus, and others, there are still remnants of
Christian faith which require them to "be true to one another"
and to maintain some kind of standard. But, as irrational man
presses the claims of the absurd on life, he forsakes all norms
for a radically irrational lawlessness. Philosophically, it means
that even a man like Heidegger, who wants no part of
irrationality still separates *thinking* from *reason*. According to
Heidegger, "Thinking only begins at the point where we have
come to know that Reason, glorified for centuries, is the most

6. Albert Camus, *The Myth of Sisyphus*, 21.

obstinate adversary of thinking."[7] A Christian can affirm this, but in a different sense, in that he affirms the priority of the absolute rationality of God to the reason of man, but Heidegger, as an existentialist, wants thinking without reason, without a pre-established pattern or necessary meaning.

In Sartre, this means that man simply is; man has being, but no essence. In Odajnyk's words, "Every man is a *tabula rasa*: he is nothing that can be defined beforehand, but must define himself through his life."[8]

In view of the studied irrationality of modern man, his cultivated barbarism, it is not surprising that lawlessness and immorality proliferate, nor that police report a growing incidence of "senseless" and "purposeless" crime. Crimes are committed for violence's sake, a defiance of reason and order, and society sees an alarming increase in anarchy. This anarchy is not the isolation of great individuals but the dissolution of all connecting ties (other than the tyrant state) between man and man. It produces, as the avantgarde dramatists of existentialism recognize, a weak man, a man who is helpless before authority and power because he is neurotic, timid, ulcer-ridden, and afraid. Wellwarth observes, with respect to the world of the dramatist Jean Tardieu,

> In Tardieu the modern mind — the mind, that is, of the ordinary man-in-the-street — craves irresponsibility and therefore willingly and uncritically, almost by now instinctively, abases itself before the first vague semblance of authority that it encounters.[9]

Except in irresponsibility and violence, modern man, according to his own philosophers, is impotent and helpless. The dramatist Eugene Ionesco portrays the moral spinelessness of man and society, and the readiness of men to justify evil rather than to oppose it. His character Berenger is given as an example of this:

[7.] Cited by William Barrett, *Irrational Man, A Study in Existential Philosophy* (Garden City, N. Y.: Doubleday Anchor Books, [1958] 1962), 206.

[8.] Walter Odajnyk, *Marxism and Existentialism* (Garden City, N. Y.: Doubleday Anchor Books, 1965), 9.

[9.] George E. Wellwarth, *The Theater of Protest and Paradox*, 93.

Having no belief of his own, he represents a society that no longer has any right to defend itself against evil because it is not convinced that it is better than the evil opposing it.[10]

The result is rebellion. In the *Ubu* plays of Alfred Jarry (1873-1907) this is rebellion on the most direct and elementary level, the scatological. It is comparable to "a child's refusal to bow to the bathroom training."[11] Jarry himself said of *Ubu Roi* that he "is an ignoble creature, which is why he is so like us all.... He is really rather a spoiled child."[12] Jarry warred against realism in the theater in the name of the new standard of rebellion. The nightmare of the inner world had to be depicted on stage. Wellwarth tells us of the development of Jarry's own principle of rebellion:

Jarry's greatest gesture of rebellion, however, was his alcoholism. There can be little doubt that he deliberately drank himself to death. Not long after his arrival in Paris, he must have made up his mind to make the supreme rebellious gesture of suicide. He chose alcohol as his medium because it was slow and because the immediate effects of the alcohol enabled him to carry on his eccentricities undisturbed by the restraints of his own personality. Alcohol freed him from himself temporarily; eventually it freed him permanently from the whole burden of his life. In a way it was a heroic death, for it was a death for a cause, and probably it was not as pleasant a one as the casual drinker might suppose. It was certainly not an insane or unreasonable death. Rebellion as Jarry saw it was a quest for total freedom and a protest against the ultimate enslavement, which is death. Jarry chose to rebel against the ultimate by systematically destroying himself. In this way he conquered — paradoxically; for, having consciously sentenced himself to death, having decided to control his own death, as it were, by deliberately bringing it on, he was able to be completely at

---

10. *Ibid.*, 67.
11. *Ibid.*, 5. For the *Ubu* plays, see Roger Shattuck and Simon Watson Taylor, eds., *Selected Works of Alfred Jarry* (New York: Grove Press, 1965), 23-63, 76-81.
12. Shattuck and Taylor, 80.

liberty, completely contemptuous of all manifestations of social order during the period of life that was left to him.[13]

Irrational man seeks an irrational end.

---

13. Wellwarth, *op. cit.*, 11.

The Death of God:
Its Implications

To all practical intent, as we have seen, Haroutunian announced "the death of God." He did not formally do so, nor did Tillich, whose thinking he echoed. This remained for Altizer and others to do. The "Death of God" school of thought was long overdue. Max Stirner, Nietzsche, and others had long before declared the death of God. Theologians were slower in doing so, not because their thinking was any more conservative, but because they had no desire to eliminate their jobs by eliminating God and the church. As a result, like Haroutunian, they spoke of "the living God" who has neither life nor non-life, neither being nor non-being.

We can be grateful to Altizer for trying to bring honesty to modern theology. The time requires, he holds, "a forthright confession of the death of the God of Christendom." The reason for the death of God and of the era of Christian civilization is *epistemological*, because "all cognitive meaning and all moral values that were once historically associated with the Christian God have collapsed." This collapse of meaning Altizer sees alternatively as a result and as a cause of the death of God. At any rate,

...we must recognize that the death of God is a historical event: God has died in *our* time, in *our* history, in *our* existence. Insofar as we live in our destiny, we can know neither a trace of God's presence nor an image of his reality. We must acknowledge, therefore, that if God has died in our history, then insofar as the church has become Christendom, insofar as the church has entered history, it has become a corpse — as Kierkegaard knew so deeply; and *all* traditional theological meaning, *all* our inherited religious meaning, is in process either of dissolution or of transformation.[1]

Altizer follows Mircea Eliade in defining modern man as the man who has negated the sacred in favor of the profane, and who regards himself as a purely historical being, without any transcendental reference or meaning.

Now by purely "historical" being Eliade means a radically profane mode of existence, a mode of existence that has withdrawn itself from an awareness of the transcendent, and immersed itself in the immediate temporal moment. This meaning of "historical" is intimately related to the modern idea of "historicity": for, in this perspective, "historicity" means a total immersion in historical time, an immersion that is totally isolated from any meaning or reality that might lie beyond it. So likewise "desacralized" cosmos means profane world, and Eliade's meaning is that modern man wills to live in a profane world, wills to know the world as profane.[2]

God is dead because modern man wills it, and "wills to live in a profane world, wills to know the world as profane." Modern man's word is the new creative word, a fiat word which kills and makes alive, ostensibly. As a part of his creative power, modern man abolished the transcendent and wills God to be dead. To cite Altizer again,

"Historical man," the man who *is* insofar as he *makes himself, within history,* is forced to identify himself with the historical moment, with "historicity," and therein

[1] Thomas J. J. Altizer, *Mircea Eliade and the Dialectic of the Sacred* (Philadelphia: Westminster Press, 1963), 13.
[2] *Ibid.,* 23.

becomes bound to a destiny that he can only know as tragic, and an existence that he can only know as absurd. By choosing a profane mode of existence — *i.e.*, by willing to abolish the transcendent — modern man has made an existential choice; he has "chosen" a tragic mode of existence, for he has "chosen" an absolute autonomy which finally encloses him within the concrete moment itself. Therefore modern man's "choice" can be realized only through the abolition of the sacred.[3]

Whether it is the writers of the literary realm or in formal philosophy and theology, modern men make much of their "tragic mode of existence." We should not take this too seriously. It is comparable to the plea of the man, who, having murdered both his father and mother, asked for mercy on the ground that he was an orphan.

Eliade himself, in discussing modern man and religion, states the case even more strongly:

> First of all, the nonreligious man refuses transcendence, accepts the relativity of "reality," and may even come to doubt the meaning of existence. The great cultures of the past too have not been entirely without nonreligious men, and it is not impossible that such men existed even on the archaic levels of culture, although as yet no testimony to their existence has come to light. But it is only in the modern societies of the West that nonreligious man has developed fully. Modern nonreligious man assumes a new existential situation; he regards himself solely as the subject and agent of history, and he refuses all appeal to transcendence. In other words, he accepts no model for humanity outside the human condition as it can be seen in the various historical situations. Man *makes himself*, and he only makes himself completely in proportion as he desacralizes himself and the world. The sacred is the prime obstacle to his freedom. He will become himself only when he is totally demysticized. He will not be truly free until he has killed the last god.[4]

---

3. *Ibid.*, 25f.
4. Mircea Eliade, *The Sacred and the Profane, The Nature of Religion* (New York: Harcourt, Brace and Company, [1957] 1959), 202f.

Man's condition is an act of choice: he "refuses transcendence" because he is determined to know only "the relativity of 'reality'" "and is prepared "to doubt the meaning of existence." In other words, man is determined to have only the world of modern epistemology, a world without God and a world without essence or meaning. The world has no meaning because it has no eternal decree of God undergirding it. Thus, the outer world is denied meaning and is reduced to a position of relativity to man, as an aspect of man's experience. Man stands alone, having no essence but only existence; but, if need be, "the meaning of existence" will also be doubted if existence should threaten to point beyond itself.

The avant-garde dramatist Eugene Ionesco is thus very much a voice of the new theology and philosophy in demanding on the one hand an acceptance of man as such, and, on the other, the freedom to be radically creative as though man were god and the sole arbiter of possibilities. Ionesco wants no savior; "saviors hate humanity, because they cannot accept it."[5] Ionesco's dramas thus do not attempt to reform or save man. His purpose is unrestricted and unchannelled creativity:

> The free development of the powers of imagination must not be restricted. There must be no canalization, no directive, no preconceived ideas, no limits. I believe a genuine work of art is one in which the initial intentions of the artist have been surpassed; where the flood of imagination has swept through the barriers or out of the narrow channels in which he first tried to confine it: extending beyond messages, ideologies and the desire to prove or to teach. This absolute freedom of the imagination is called escape or evasion by the gloomy critics of our time whereas it is true creation. To make a new world is to satisfy the insistent demands of a mind that would be stifled if its needs were not fulfilled.[6]

Creation is irrational and emotional for Ionesco. "Creation implies total liberty. It is an entirely different procedure from

---

[5.] Eugene Ionesco, *Notes and Counter Notes, Writings on the Theatre* (New York: Grove Press, 1964), 123.
[6.] *Ibid.*, 124.

that involved in conceptual thought.... When I write a play, I have no idea what it is going to be like. I have my ideas *afterward.* At the start, there is nothing but an emotional state."[7] Ionesco should be happy as a new god, but he is in fact miserable. "I am dying myself, and nothing remains of nothing."[8] He is "aware of the impossibility of communication" and feels alone.[9]

The freedom of man from God becomes man's new slavery. The goal of modern man is freedom from God, the goal set before him by the tempter in the beginning (Genesis 3:1-5). For the existentialist, man makes himself. Man has no essence, no pre-established nature, only being, until he, by his own choice, defines himself. Until man makes himself, he is "indefinable," because he is as yet "nothing." "Man is nothing else but what he makes of himself."[10]

This freedom and power have serious consequences, Sartre says:

> ...Dostoievsky said, "If God didn't exist, everything would be possible." That is the very starting point of existentialism. Indeed, everything is permissible if God does not exist, and as a result man is forlorn, because neither within him nor without does he find anything to cling to. He can't start making excuses for himself.

> If existence really does precede essence, there is no explaining things away by reference to a fixed and given human nature. In other words, there is no determinism, man is free, man is freedom. On the other hand, if God does not exist, we find no values or commands to turn to which legitimize our conduct. So, in the bright realm of values, we have no excuses behind us, nor justification before us. We are alone, with no excuses.

> That is the idea I shall try to convey when I say that man is condemned to be free. Condemned, because he did not create himself, yet, in other respects is free; because, once

---

[7.] *Ibid.,* 129.

[8.] *Ibid.,* 216.

[9.] *Ibid.,* 227.

[10.] Jean-Paul Sartre, *Existentialism and Human Emotions* (New York: Philosophical Library, 1957), 15.

thrown into the world, he is responsible for everything he does.[11]

Here again a murderous orphan tugs at our heart strings.

Freedom, however, has a severe limitation; it is in fact negated by the certainty of death. Death is not man's choice, Sartre recognizes. For the Christian, it comes at God's appointed hour and as an aspect of God's determined purpose. But, for the existentialist, "If death is not the free determination of our being, it cannot complete our life." For the existentialist, it is "the sequences of the universe" which determine death. "If this is the case, we can no longer even say that death confers a meaning on life from the outside; a meaning can only come from subjectivity. Since death does not appear on the foundation of our freedom, it can only remove all meaning from life."[12] We can understand now why Alfred Jarry, to assert his freedom, willed his death while still a young man. It was an attempt to assert a god-like determination over his own being. As Sartre recognized, "the very existence of *death* alienates us wholly in our own life to the advantage of the Other."[13] We can understand also why modern science is so determined to conquer death and to make man his own god.[14] However, Sartre holds, by recognizing death for what it is we can be freed from "its so-called constraint." By accepting freedom, we accept finitude. "The very act of freedom is therefore the assumption and creation of finitude. If I make myself, I make myself finite and hence my life is unique."[15] (For all his existentialism, at this point Sartre joined Margaret Fuller [1810-1850] in accepting the universe.)

For Sartre, "man is the being whose project is to be God." "To be man means to reach toward being God. Or if you prefer, man fundamentally is the desire to be God." This

---

[11.] *Ibid.*, 22f.

[12.] Jean-Paul Sartre, *Being and Nothingness, An Essay in Phenomenological Ontology*, Hazel E. Barnes, trans. (New York: Philosophical Library, 1956). 538f.

[13.] *Ibid.*, 543.

[14.] See Bolton Davidheiser, *To Be As God* (Nutley, New Jersey.: Presbyterian and Reformed Publishing Co., 1972).

[15.] Sartre, *op. cit.*, 546.

presents a contradiction. Sartre had said that man has no essence, no pre-determined nature, but now he defines man's nature as the desire to be God; "man is the being whose project is to be God." Sartre is aware of this problem:

> It may be asked, if man on coming into the world is borne toward God as toward his limit, if he can choose only to be God, what becomes of freedom. For freedom is nothing other than a choice which creates for itself its own possibilities, but it appears here that the initial project of being God, which "defines" man, comes close to being the same as a human "nature" or an "essence."[16]

Sartre's attempts to escape this dilemma are not our present concern. We must note in passing that Sartre sees man's attempt to become God a futile one, "for man loses himself as man in order that God may be born. But the idea of God is contradictory and we lose ourselves in vain. Man is a useless passion."[17] Previously, Sartre had identified freedom with "nihilation"; he declared this to be a *strict* identification. "The only being which can be called free is the being which nihilates its being. Moreover we know that nihilation is *lack of being* and can not be otherwise. Freedom is precisely the being which makes itself a lack of being."[18] If this seems to resemble the world of Alfred Jarry and Dostoievsky's Kirilov, it is because it does.

What concerns us in all this is that the death of God means also the death of man. Some existentialists have seen this. Malraux wrote, "For you absolute reality has been God, then man. But *man is dead*, after God...." According to Knight,

> Malraux was one of the first to see that the "death of God" involves that of Man. God understood not only as Deity, but as any principle purporting to render the universe intelligible: "Europe is dominated by the idea, more or less clearly defined, of the impossibility of grasping any reality whatever." Despite the loss of all the "coherent myths"

---

16. *Ibid.*, 566.
17. *Ibid.*, 615.
18. *Ibid.*, 567.

with which Europe has attempted to domesticate that universe, she clings desperately to a conception which is nonsense without them — that of the "inner world," of the individual *per se*.[19]

Michel Foucault has gone further: he has proclaimed the death of man. In speaking of the coming death of man,

> Naturally he does not mean that real people may soon be wiped out. His reference is to the liberal humanist's *conception* of man — man regarded as the uniquely proper center for the organization of knowledge and as a coherent, free, active essence in the universe. Foucault maintains that "man" in this philosophical sense is "a sort of image correlative with God" and "an invention" of a surprisingly recent date, rendered possible by the cultural pattern that emerged in Europe around the beginning of the nineteenth century.[20]

Gunther Stent believes that the actual disappearance of civilization as we know it is a great possibility, but Foucault sees the death of man in another sense. It is the godlike man of humanism who is dying.

> Each distinct cultural period, Foucault says, conceals beneath its surface a characteristic "system," or "structure," which he chooses to designate by the Greek term for knowledge, *episteme*. *Episteme* appears to have such a subtle mode of existence that it cannot be defined directly. Like poetry, it has to be sniffed out by examples and trapped by obliqueness. Foucault refers to it several times as merely a tendency toward certain ways of knowing, "an archeological network," as the "space" in which knowledge occurs, as a "historical a priori," and as whatever it is that "defines the conditions for the possibility of all knowledge."[21]

We are now at the end of an epistemological tradition, and the man created by humanistic epistemology is now dying. We are now in the process of finding a new and non-humanistic

---

19. E. W. Knight, *Literature Considered as Philosophy*, 182.
20. Roy McMullen, "Michel Foucault," in *Horizon* XI, 4 (Autumn, 1969), 37.
21. *Ibid.*, 37f.

epistemology, Foucault believes. There is no evidence that what Foucault wants is a Christian epistemology.

In any case, we have seen that the epistemology of modern man has had devastating effects on philosophy, religion, culture, and society. The everyday life of man has been altered and warped. In the modern world view, "we are given a religion of killing in place of a religion of a rising from the dead."[22]

By abolishing God from his philosophy, man dreamed that he was freeing himself for a glorious golden age in which man would be free to re-enter paradise on his own terms. Instead of gaining paradise, man has turned the earth into hell and seeks an escape into the realm of hallucinatory drugs. By means of his philosophy as well as by his drugs, Stent points out,

> ...the boundary between the real and the imagined has been dissolved. For the hippies, the reality principle is all but dead. This overt erosion of the reality principle embodied in the hippies was not, of course, invented in the Haight-Ashbury district. On the contrary, the philosophical basis of reality has been the subject of critical discussions for some two hundred years, ever since Immanuel Kant claimed that, in the last analysis, the real world is a subjective concept rather than an objective fact. The transcendentalist world picture of the present avant garde artists, mentioned in the preceding chapter, is evidently another latter-day reflection of this trend to lessen the importance of distinguishing between the real and the imagined. The lessening of this distinction appears also to be the theme of such latter-day films as Resnais' *Last Year at Marienbad* and Antonioni's *Blow-Up*. But the novelty of the hippies consists in their being the first large-scale community in the West which actually *acts* according to these ideas.[23]

The result will be, according to Stent, a gradual decay of civilization to the point that we will recreate Polynesia on a global scale, men living in terms of pleasure rather than reality.

[22.] Nicholas Berdyaev, *Dostoievsky* (New York: Meridian Books, [1934] (1957), 153.
[23.] Gunther S. Stent, *The Coming of the Golden Age*, 136.

The novelist Broch, in his trilogy, *The Sleepwalkers*, portrayed the disintegration of modern man and his culture as a product of epistemology. In an "Epistemological Excursus" it is apparent why Broch called his work "a philosophical essay." Broch was intensely aware of the disintegration of values:

> Can this age be said to have reality? Does it possess any real value in which the meaning of its existence is preserved? Is there a reality for the non-meaning of a non-existence? In what haven has reality found its refuge? In science, in law, in duty or in the uncertainty of an ever-questioning logic whose point of plausibility has vanished into the infinite? Hegel called history "the path to the liberation of spiritual substance," the path leading to the self-liberation of the spirit, and it has become the path leading to the self-destruction of all values.[24]

There is now, Broch said, "a contempt for all philosophy, a weariness of words," as men despair of any answer. Man faces very urgent questions, such as, "what is an historical event? what is historical unity? or, to go still further: what is an event at all? what principle of selection must be followed to weld single occurrences into the unity of an event?" Man has trouble phrasing his questions because of his "complete mistrust" even of words. The world of philosophy and of modern man has been divided into a world of nature, unaffected by values, and a philosophy of spirit, conditioned by values. "The first declared bankruptcy of philosophy" was to confine "the identity of Thought and Being to the realm of logic and mathematics."[25] In other words, the world of brute factuality was separated from reason or thought.

Broch's solution was to return to an earlier form of the dialectic and to hold that "the world is a product of the intelligible Self, for the Platonic idea has never been abandoned nor ever can be."[26] He did call for a systematic philosophy and

---

24. Hermann Broch, *The Sleepwalkers, A Trilogy* (London: Martin Secker, 1932), 559.
25. *Ibid.,* 560f.
26. *Ibid.,* 563.

religion, declaring that "The total system of a religion makes the world that it dominates a rational world..."; but he still held to "the independent sovereignty of reason." He recognized "the disintegration of values" when man is left to his own "empiric autonomy," but he sought to link autonomy to Platonic ideas and regain a unity of meaning.[27]

There has thus been no lack of awareness on the part of the modern man as to the consequences of his epistemology. They terrify and disintegrate his being. Modern man has given us a more vivid picture of his own despair than we can ever rival. Terrifying as the nightmare of his existence is, it is the world of his own choosing. He prefers it to life under God. He is still like the murderer, who, having killed father and mother, weeps in self-pity because he is an orphan. But he knows what he is doing, and why he is doing it. Man the sinner would rather blind himself than, seeing, to see God.

---

27. *Ibid.*, 628.

8

Authority and Knowledge

When men discuss epistemology, it is their desire to be as "objective" and "scientific" as possible, and to convey the impression that theirs is a concern with conclusions open to all men by any fair standards. The most reprehensible position for them is one which offers itself as an infallible truth, to be accepted on authority. They will assure you that it is precisely this kind of dogmaticism in Christianity that repels reasonable men. The goal of philosophical and scientific inquiry should be clearly ascertainable facts which are open to all thinking men. The conclusions should be readily provable or open to testing and verification in order to be acceptable.

The offense of Biblical faith has been its radically divergent position. Instead of beginning with man and man's reason, it begins with God and His revelation. Instead of bringing all things to the judgment bar of man's mind, it takes all things to the infallible word of God for a standard. The humanist regards such an appeal as the ultimate in intellectual bankruptcy and as a kind of scholarly obscenity.

More than a few churchmen have agreed with the enemies of the faith at this point. They insist that they accept the authority of God's word; they do regard it as valid knowledge, but only because it meets the requirements of their reason and Aristotle's logic. Thus, Carnell declared,

> Granted that we need revelation from God to learn how He will dispose of us at the end of our lives, are there not many revelations which vie for our approval? How shall we make a selection, when we are not God? We can answer this in a sentence: Accept that revelation which, when examined, yields a system of thought which is horizontally self-consistent and which vertically fits the facts of history. When viewing the Bible, the Christian says, "I see a series of data in the Bible. If I accept the system as it is outlined, I can make a lot of problems easy." Bring on your revelations! Let them make peace with the law of contradiction and the facts of history, and they will deserve a rational man's assent. A careful examination of the Bible reveals that it passes these stringent examinations *summa cum laude*.[1]

A number of comments can be made about this sorry statement. To cite a few, *first*, Carnell manifested a curious view of Scripture, if our "need" for it is "to learn how He will dispose of us at the end of our lives." This is a humanistic approach and misses the entire thrust of Scripture. *Second*, there are *not* "many revelations which vie for our approval," Carnell to the contrary. Prior to the Christian era, there was no purported revelation outside the Scriptures. What we call "the sacred books of the East" made no claim for themselves that is comparable to the idea of revelation. Since these books did not begin with a sovereign and omnipotent God, they had no word coming from such a God. The "sacred books of the East" are religious and philosophical writings, some of them atheistic, but they are not revelations. Only after the beginning of the Christian era do we get ostensible revelations, in clear imitation of Scripture, such as the Koran and the Book of Mormon. The idea of a revealed word is Biblical. Only a sovereign, omnipotent, predestinating God can speak an

---

[1] Edward John Carnell, *An Introduction to Christian Apologetics* (Grand Rapids: Eerdmans, 1952), 178.

infallible word, and the idea of such a God and such a word is not present outside the Biblical tradition.

Third, and most important, ultimacy and authority in Carnell's system rest in "a rational man's assent," in the supposedly autonomous reason of man. What of that man's sin and his radical hostility of God, his unwillingness to acknowledge God in any form or manner? Man's reason is clearly affected by his sin and is used in man's warfare against God. Carnell's god is clearly not sovereign. The test of rationality is not the absolute rationality of God but the fallen reason of man. The God and the Bible who pass Carnell's test *summa cum laude* are not the God and the Bible of Christian orthodoxy.

How true this judgment of Carnell is appeared in his study of *Christian Commitment, An Apologetic* (1957). It made no mention of the Bible, of its inspiration as a means of knowledge and a source of moral law. It is an exercise in existentialism and is an unhappy and painfully embarrassing effort. Initiative in salvation is given to man, which is consistent with the primacy of authority given to man's reason. "The minimal elements in fellowship oblige us to believe that God is under the same necessity to extend his life to the humble as he is to withhold it from the proud."[2] Carnell does not seem to be aware that necessity outlaws grace. If man can compel God to a necessary action, then man is sovereign.

All of Carnell's efforts to play the rationalistic game added only to the credit of the humanists rather than to the cause of Christ. For the philosopher is first of all a creature made in God's image who is either in obedience to God or in revolt against Him. We have seen how radically religious the presuppositions of epistemology are. They begin, not with "the facts" but with an act of faith.

Hear Max Stirner begin and end with an affirmation of absolute and ultimate authority, infallible authority:

---

[2] Edward John Carnell, *Christian Commitment, An Apologetic* (New York: Macmillan, 1957), 251.

...To the Christian the world's history is the higher thing, because it is the history of Christ or "man"; to the egoist only *his* history has value, because he wants to develop only *himself*, not the mankind-idea, not God's plan, not the purposes of Providence, not liberty, and the like. He does not look upon himself as a tool of the idea or a vessel of God, he recognizes no calling, he does not fancy that he exists for the future development of mankind and that he must contribute his mite to it, but he lives himself out, careless of how well or ill humanity may fare thereby...

They say of God, "Names name thee not." That holds good of me: no *concept* expresses me, nothing that is designated as my essence exhausts me; they are only names. Likewise they say of God that he is perfect and has no calling to strive after perfection. That too holds good of me alone.

I am *owner* of my might, and I am so when I know myself as *unique*. In the *unique one* the owner himself returns into his creative nothing, out of which he is born. Every higher essence above me, be it God, be it man, weakens the feeling of my uniqueness, and pales only before the sun of this consciousness. If I concern myself for myself, the unique one, then my concern rests on its transitory, mortal creator, who consumes himself, and I may say:

All things are nothing to me.[3]

Stirner, as an anarchist who believed in the ultimacy and absolute authority of his own will, had only contempt for atheists who were afraid to practice incest or bigamy. These men are still Christians, he held, because they acknowledge a law above their will, and a word beyond their word.[4]

Can we say that Freud, who shattered the idea of rational man, broke with the idea of an ultimate authority or word? True enough, Freud regarded reason as fraudulent in its claims and as a façade for dark, subterranean forces in man, but when we examine Freud's doctrine of the unconscious, we find another form of the humanistic doctrine of infallibility.

[3.] Max Stirner, *The Ego and His Own* (New York: Modern Library, n.d.), 386f.
[4.] *Ibid.*, 47f.

Freud's unconscious cannot lie. It is a perpetually true and pure spring of truth that wells up out of the hidden nature of man. Man's id knows no inhibition in itself. It tells the truth, and the only problem a man has is to locate the proper psychoanalytic interpreter of his private well of infallibility.

In an earlier era, men talked naively, and in semi-biblical language, of the divine right of kings, or of parliament, and some still talk of the divine right of the people (*vox populi, vox dei*). Now the same doctrine of infallibility has a more sophisticated and a disguised format, but the content is the same.

Let us turn again to Sartre as he writes on epistemology:

> The world is human. We can see the very particular position of consciousness: being is everywhere, opposite me, around me; it weighs down on me, it besieges me, and I am perpetually referred from being to being; that table which is there is being and *nothing* else. I want to grasp this being, and I no longer find anything but *myself*. This is because knowledge, intermediate between being and non-being, refers me to absolute being if I want to make knowledge subjective and refers me to myself when I think to grasp the absolute. The very meaning of knowledge is what it is not and is not what it is; for in order to know being such as it is, it would be necessary to be that being. But there is this "such as it is" only because I am not the being which I know; and if I should become it, then the "such as it is" would vanish and could no longer even be thought. We are not dealing here either with scepticism — which supposes precisely that the *such as it is* belongs to being — nor with relativism. Knowledge puts us in the presence of the absolute, and there is a truth of knowledge. But this truth, although releasing to us nothing more and nothing less than the absolute, remains strictly human.[5]

"Knowledge puts us in the presence of the absolute, and there is a truth of knowledge." Sartre gets no further than himself, existential man, in his "knowledge." Where existential man is ultimate, "all human activities are equivalent." Man must free

---

[5.] Sartre, *Being and Nothingness*, 218.

himself from external goals, from the idea of "values as transcendent givens independent of human subjectivity." In fact, "it amounts to the same thing whether one gets drunk alone or is a leader of nations."[6]

Philosophy offers us simply an alternate authority, another word and another reason in the stead of God's absolute rationality and God's infallible word. Infallibility is not denied: it is transferred and concealed. Authority is not replaced by reason and science but simply transferred to reason and science, asking us to bow down before new gods, and to question them not, since they are by definition the essence of reason and true knowledge. The new breed of prophets gives us, with the utmost aplomb, their new word and asks us to bow before it, or to think only in terms of it. Max Planck declared, "Whatever can be measured exists." This is not a conclusion but a presupposition, and it tells us how we are permitted to investigate reality, and also what reality is, i.e., that which can be measured. A. Einstein, B. Podolsky, and N. Rosen, in writing on "Can Quantum Mechanical Description of Physical Reality Be Considered Complete?," in *Physical Review*, vol. 47 (1935), p. 777, stated:

> The elements of the physical reality cannot be determined by *a priori* philosophical considerations, but must be found by an appeal to results of experiments and measurements. A comprehensive definition of reality, is, however, unnecessary for our purpose. We shall be satisfied with the following criterion, which we regard as reasonable. If, without in any way disturbing a system, we can predict with certainty (i.e. with probability equal to unity) the value of a physical quantity, then there exists an element of physical reality corresponding to this physical quality.[7]

These men have not, like Stirner, declared themselves to be infallible. They have declared that "the elements of physical reality" cannot be discovered or determined by "*a priori*

---

6. *Ibid.*, 626f.
7. Cited in Levi, *Philosophy and the Modern World*, 557.

philosophical considerations," and certainly not by religious consideration. This latter is so preposterous they feel no need to mention it. We are asked to think that their thinking is *a posteriori*, after the facts, a reasoning from the facts to causes rather than vice versa. Christian thinking which is faithful to its premises is neither *a priori* nor *a posteriori*, because it sees both causes and facts as derivative from the sovereign and ontological Trinity who is the maker of all things. Having renounced *a priori* thinking and philosophy, these men then give us a "reasonable" criterion, an *a priori* conclusion and a presupposition. Basic to that criterion is a concept of reality as measurable and a closed system in terms of that. Within that closed system, there are openings for many possibilities, but the door is authoritatively and infallibly closed to the sovereign God of Scripture. The fundamental presupposition of the world view of these men is as authoritatively committed against the ontological Trinity as Scripture is to the triune God. There can be, with scientists, polite palaver to the effect that God is an open question, but their presuppositions and methodology ensure that God cannot be considered. While operating on the assumption of a world which is rational and orderly because it is undergirded by the eternal decree of God, they insist on speaking of chance and probability rather than anything which points to and presupposes God.

The *given*, the presupposition, in any system of thought is held to be authoritatively and infallibly true. Reality is defined in terms of the presupposition, and all reasoning is circular reasoning in terms of what is implicit in the *given*. The thinking of the Greek philosophers is riddled with mysticism, occultism, and esoteric concepts. Aristotle had a public doctrine in his writings and an esoteric one for his pupils, and he assured Alexander the Great that the published writings did not reveal the secret doctrine.[8] However, we are solemnly assured that "reason" and science were born with the Greeks because their premises were radically humanistic. This is the

---

[8] Benjamin Farrington, *Greek Science, Its Meaning For Us* (Penguin Books, [1944] 1949), II, 156.

criterion of rationality, humanism. The hidden doctrine of modern thought conceals its infallible faith that God cannot exist, i.e., the God of Scripture. The other side of the coin is that the ultimate authority is scientific man.

Our politics today is the politics of infallibility. Dewey's idea of the Great Community, the ideas of the democratic consensus, and the Marxist concept of the dictatorship of the proletariat all have as their presupposition a doctrine of the infallibility of an elite group who represent the general will. The immediate source of this doctrine is in Jean-Jacques Rousseau (1712-1778), who held that *"the general will is always right and ever tends to the public advantage."*[9] All the murderous arrogance of modern political man stems from this doctrine of infallibility. All the attempts of the scientific and intellectual elite to rule man stem from their belief that they are this voice of the general will.

The doctrine of infallibility does not disappear when men deny it to God and His Word; it accrues to men. In the hands of men it becomes a doctrine of oppression.

Thus, we need not apologize for the doctrine of infallibility, nor for an appeal to authority. These are common to every school of thought, and it is dishonesty to deny it. Carnell's appeal was to reason, to his existential being as expressed therein. Stirner bowed low before his ego, scientists to themselves and their methodology, and the modern world in its political and social life to the general will. As a result of the doctrine of the general will, man has become group-oriented, and his standards and tastes are derived from the group.

Octavius Brooks Frothingham (1822-1895), a thinker of the Religion of Humanity, expressed plainly the essence of *modernism* as a belief in the infallibility of the hour and its demands. His "God" was Hegel's world-soul expressing itself in every historical era and having no law or standard beyond the hour, so that the historical moment was and is the infallible

---

9. J. J. Rousseau, "The Social Contract," Book II, chapter III, in Sir Ernest Barker, ed., *Social Contract, Essays by Locke, Hume, and Rousseau* (London: Oxford University Press, [1947] 1958), 274.

voice of history, "God," or spirit. Of course, what that inner meaning or expression of the historical moment is depends on the elite thinkers. According to Frothingham, on the infallibility of the historical hour,

> The interior spirit of any age is the spirit of God; and no faith can be living that has that spirit against it; no Church can be strong except in that alliance. The life of the time appoints the creed of the time and modifies the establishment of the time.[10]

This is the faith of modernism in religion, politics, the sciences, the arts, and every other area. The creeds all have their moment of truth, and they then pass on. Yesterday's truth cannot be considered seriously today. Honor Calvin indeed, or Augustine, Aquinas, or Luther, for each expressed the truth of their hour, but pass on to the present and its needs. To separate ourselves from the infallible historical moment is death or at best irrelevance. As Frothingham stated it,

> Humanity has but one life, breathes but one atmosphere, draws sustenance from one central orb. To be reconciled with humanity, to feel the common pulse, is life; to be alienated from humanity, to have no share in the common vitality, is death. The slightest material separation is felt disastrously.[11]

Isaiah had a better word: "Cease ye from man, whose breath is in his nostrils: for wherein is he to be accounted of?" (Isaiah 2:22).

[10.] O. B. Frothingham, *The Religion of Humanity*, 3rd ed. (New York: G. P. Putnam's Sons, 1875), 7f.

[11.] *Ibid.*, 130.

9

Ultimate Authority

As we have seen, Frothingham held to the infallibility of the historical hour, so that, as men gave themselves to the "interior spirit" of their age, they gave themselves to the truth of the hour and were the expression of the spirit of history. For Rousseau, the general will in its moment by moment expressions gives the infallible truth for the moment. For Sartre, the drunk is the expression of his existential moment and is beyond criticism or judgment.

Clearly, this is a doctrine of infallibility, but a very different one than the doctrine of Scripture. It is necessarily so. Humanism must have a for-the-moment infallibility. It cannot have an infallible truth which is valid from age to age, or from year to year. To have such a truth, law, or value would be to place it above and beyond men, and to make it binding on all generations. Such a concept of truth is death to humanism; it denies the ultimacy of man and of man's word. It is necessary, if man is to be ultimate and infallible, for man to speak *the free word for the moment*, the existential truth. According to von Fersen existential philosophy "determines the worth of knowledge not in relation to truth but according to its biological value contained in the pure data of unconsciousness when unaffected by emotions, volitions, and social prejudices. Both the source and the elements of knowledge are sensations as they 'exist' in our consciousness. There is no difference between the external and internal worlds, as there is no natural phenomenon which could not be examined psychologically; it has its 'existence' in states of the mind."[1] Only as a man frees himself from all save the existential moment can he express the infallible truth of the moment. Man can have no tie to anything save to his biology, his existence. Since existential man cannot arrest history, eliminate death, or halt all change, the only infallible word which he can have is the word of his being, his existence, *the word of flux.* The more radically man gives himself to this word of flux, the more infallible he is. Hence the intense striving for continual novelty and change in the art of modern man. If in all his being and work he fails to show this radical commitment to change, he has missed the voice of truth, the word of flux. The word of man is necessarily the word of flux, and modern thought is consistent to its premises in seeking its gospel and infallibility in flux.

The word of God, on the other hand, is necessarily the certain and unchanging word true for all times, and infallibly so. Because the God of Scripture is the sovereign uncreated Being who is the maker of all things, He is beyond flux. "For I am the LORD, I change not" (Malachi 3:6). God is totally self-conscious. There are no dark corners in His being, nor is there any aspect of creation outside the totality of His government and decree. In Revelation 4:6 all creation is like a sea of glass, clear as crystal, before the throne of God. All creation is open before Him, its totality of life from beginning to end being but aspects of His eternal decree.[2] In God, moreover, potentiality and actuality are one: there are no unrealized potentialities in Him. God is "He Who Is," or "I AM THAT I AM" (Exodus 3:14) the self-existent and absolute Lord of all things. The universe is His creation, brought into

---

[1.] Sigmar von Fersen, "Existential Philosophy," in Dagovert D. Runes, ed., *Dictionary of Philosophy*, 15th ed., rev. (New York: Philosophical Library, 1960), 102f.

[2.] See R. J. Rushdoony, *Thy Kingdom Come* (Nutley, N. J.: Presbyterian and Reformed Publishing Co., 1971), 129-135.

being by His creative word, and governed from its first day to the last totally by God in terms of His eternal counsel. "Known unto God are all his works from the beginning of the world" (Acts 15:18). His government and counsel are total. "Are not two sparrows sold for a farthing? and one of them shall not fall on the ground without your Father. But the very hairs of your head are all numbered. Fear ye not therefore, ye are of more value than many sparrows" (Matthew 10:29-31).

Such a God, being sovereign, omniscient, omnipotent, and absolute, can *only* speak an infallible word. Because God has total knowledge and absolutely governs all things, His word is of necessity the infallible word. If all creation and all history were not controlled by the sovereign God, then an infallible word would be impossible. Moreover, if history and nature are not entirely and wholly governed by the plan of God, neither knowledge nor the sciences would be possible. There would be no essential dependability to anything. Just as the word of "infallible" man is the word of flux, so the science of such a world would be a science of flux. If brute factuality and change govern all things, then, if total knowledge were possible at any given moment, it would not be valid knowledge in the next moment. However, the moment itself would give no valid knowledge, since brute factuality would be impervious to rational understanding or classification.

Scripture thus is self-attesting. As Van Til has so well stated it,

> ...There would be no reasonably reliable method of identifying the Word of God in human history unless human history is controlled by God. The doctrine of Scripture as self-attesting presupposes that whatsoever comes to pass in history does so by virtue of the plan and counsel of the living God. If everything happens by virtue of the plan of God then all created reality, every aspect of it, is inherently revelational of God and of his plan. All facts of history are what they are ultimately because of what God intends and makes them to be. Even that which is accomplished in human history through the instrumentality of men still happens by virtue of the plan of

God. God tells the stars by their names. He identifies by complete description. He knows exhaustively. He knows exhaustively because He controls completely.

Of such a God it is that the Bible speaks. So it is once again a matter of going about in circles. It is impossible to attain to the idea of such a God by speculation independently of Scripture. It has never been done and is inherently impossible. Such a God must identify himself. Such a God it is, and only such a God, who identifies all the facts of the universe. And in identifying all the facts of the universe he sets these facts in relation to one another.[3]

The self-attesting word of man is exactly that, it attests to the self. The most it can attest to is the "I," the experiencing self of man, and it cannot account for that. Apart from the God of Scripture, facts become only brute facts and nothing more. The facts of Scripture and the facts of nature and history are alike understandable only in terms of the presupposition of the God of Scripture and His infallible word. For a man to be consistent to the premise of unbelief means to deny all possibility of knowledge because brute factuality is impervious to rationality. Van Til, who has so powerfully set forth the Christian theory of knowledge, has said that

> ...There can therefore be no fact which is ultimately out of accord with the system of truth set forth in Scripture. Every fact in the universe is what it is just because of the place that it has in the system.

> Moreover, to say that every fact in the world is what it is because of its place in the system of truth set forth in Scripture is to establish the legitimacy of the Christian principle of discontinuity. The system of truth set forth in Scripture cannot be fully understood by the creature. The point is that man as finite cannot understand God his Maker in an exhaustive manner. And as he cannot understand God exhaustively, so he cannot understand anything related to God in an exhaustive way. And all things are related to God.

---

3. Cornelius Van Til, *Christian Theory of Knowledge*, 14; 1969 ed., 28.

The objections against the phenomena of Scripture would therefore be legitimate if those who make them could show the positive foundation on which they stand in making them...

Now it is of course true that many of the sciences do not, like theology proper, concern themselves directly with the question of religion. Granting this it remains a matter of great significance that ultimately all the facts of the universe are either what they are because of their relation to the system of truth set forth in Scripture or they ar not. In every discussion about every fact, therefore, it is the two principles, that of the believer in Scripture and that of the non-Christian, that stand over against one another. Both principles are totalitarian. Both claim all the facts. And it is in the light of this point that the relation of the Bible as the infallible word of God and the "facts" of science and history must finally be understood.[4]

The mind of man can never comprehend the nature of God exhaustively. We can know God truly, because God is true to Himself, totally self-consistent, but we can never know Him exhaustively. We are but creatures, and He is the Creator. While God's absolute rationality undergirds all things, man's reason and logic, being finite, can never know exhaustively that universe, let alone the Being of God. Moreover, sin makes Scripture necessary, for that knowledge of God which is possible to the mind of man (Romans 1:18-21), man suppresses or holds down in unrighteousness. The problem of knowledge is complicated and governed by the fact of sin. "So far as the natural man thinks self-consciously according to his principle as a sinner he cannot accept the analysis that God gives in his word."[5]

The perspicuity of Scripture, the belief that Scripture sets forth clearly and simply the truth of God, that man is a sinner and how God removes his sin, is basic to Christian epistemology. "But this idea of perspicuity or clarity is not opposed to the 'incomprehensibility' of God. The system of

---

[4.] *Ibid.*, 21f; 1969 ed., 35ff.
[5.] *Ibid.*, 35; 1969 ed., 55.

Scripture is an analogical system. The relation between God and man is in the nature of the case not exhaustively expressible in human language."[6]

The rationalism of the fallen man is his insistence that there can be no absolute God to whom he must be in subjection and who absolutely governs man and the world. This rationalism demands a perspicuity in which all reality, and whatever gods may be, are totally and exhaustively knowable by man. All things must be penetrable by human logic.

On the other hand, fallen man is also irrationalistic. He insists that reality cannot be controlled by the sovereign plan of God. It cannot be a universe of law governed by a Creator who exists apart from and beyond the world. The world must be "open" to the new because it has no plan and is in perpetual flux. Brute facts change in terms of no pre-established pattern but merely as an aspect of an open universe, open to total flux or change. Such a position is an assertion of a radical irrationalism. Both the rationalism and irrationalism of modern man are aspects of his argument against God. God cannot be the God of Scripture: He does not meet the requirement of being totally penetrable by man's logic. On the other hand, the absolutely rational eternal plan of God cannot be true because the universe is irrational and not governed by reason and law. The mystery required in Christian faith is there because the finite mind of man cannot grasp the absolute rationality of God: it is incomprehensible to man's finite reason. Man's reason, however, can know God and the universe truly, although not exhaustively. For modern man, mystery means irrationality. However, as he levels these same charges against the Christian, his ground appears all the more clearly, i.e., his own ultimacy. Turning again to Van Til's telling analysis,

> In terms of this rationalism he must therefore deny that any system can be called perspicuous or clear that is not open to complete inspection by man. To be sure, the

6. *Ibid.*, 46; 1969 ed., 68.

natural man does not mind if it takes many thousands or millions of years before reality should be exhaustively stated. What he objects to is the idea of the mind of God as inherently incomprehensible to man, because self-sufficient and therefore independent.

On the other hand the natural man, as indicated repeatedly, insists that reality is ultimately "open." It constantly produces the wholly new. It cannot then be controlled by a plan of a God who exists apart from the world. God himself must, together with the world and as an aspect of the world, be involved in a process or he cannot be honored as God. So the idea of a system of truth such as orthodox Christianity pretends to have, a system which clearly, in readily identifiable and in directly available fashion, tells man what is true and what he ought to do, cannot exist. We must think of mystery as something ultimate, as something that involves God as well as man. This idea of mystery as inclusive of God as well as man is taken as correlative to the notion that all reality, again inclusive of both God and man, is exhaustively lit up and wholly penetrable to man. The two notions must be taken as supplementative of one another. Only then, says modern man, do we do justice to both aspects of reality, its wholly hidden and its wholly revealed character.[7]

The perspective of would-be autonomous man is hostile to an autonomous, self-attesting word of God. He will not submit to the idea that the Bible gives man God's truth whereby man must know himself and the world around him. The ideas of a self-contained God and of His infallible word are repellent to him.

These ideas will therefore be charged with being both irrationalistic and rationalistic by those who make man the final reference point in predication.

1. They will be said to be irrationalistic in terms of what is actually the rationalistic notion of fallen man. Fallen man putting himself virtually in the place of God also virtually demands essential continuity between himself and God.

[7.] *Ibid.*, 47; 1969 ed., 68f.

He speaks of thought in general and of the laws of being
in general. He therewith subjects the thought and being of
God to the same limitations to which man is subject. In
consequence the Christian's view of Scripture appears to it
as breaking the continuity between God and man, as being
irrationalistic.

2. On the other hand, the Biblical idea of self-
identification and as containing the ultimate system of
truth will be charged with being rationalistic by the
natural man. This is the case because such an idea of
Scripture involves the notion that God knows all things
because he controls all things. Thus, it is argued, the
sacredness of human personality and human freedom
would be violated. In the name of the ideal of science —
the ideal of complete comprehension and continuity —
the idea of Scripture is said to be irrationalistic. In the
name of personality — the idea of freedom — the idea of
Scripture is said to be rationalistic.[8]

Whenever and wherever the authority of Scripture is to any
degree undermined or diluted, it is in order to make room for
the claims of autonomous man. To the degree that the
necessity, the perspicuity, and the authority of Scripture are
rejected, to that degree the iceberg of autonomous man's
epistemology begins to loom above the surface. Autonomous
man wants an "open" universe in which man and God (or the
gods) are alike subject to the same conditions, so that no
advantage accrues to God. A god who is not the Creator and
determiner of all things but a senior being or citizen of the
universe is not inescapably revealed in all creation. "The
heavens declare the glory of God; and the firmament sheweth
his handywork. Day unto day uttereth speech, and night unto
night sheweth knowledge. There is no speech nor language,
where their voice is not heard" (Psalm 19:1-3). Such a God
cannot be hidden. Man tries continually to suppress that
witness (Romans 1:18-21), but it cannot be silenced.

If I ascend up into heaven, thou art there: if I make my bed
in hell, behold, thou art there.

[8.] *Ibid.*, 48; 1969 ed., 70.

If I take the wings of the morning, and dwell in the
uttermost parts of the sea;
Even there shall thy hand lead me, and thy right hand shall
hold me. (Psalm 139:8-10)

The God of Scripture is not a hidden God, but neither is He
wholly revealed, because His inexhaustible and incomprehensible Being are beyond the ability of finite man to
comprehend or know exhaustively.

On the other hand, the god of Karl Barth is both wholly
revealed and wholly hidden.[9] Because he is not the creator and
governor of all things, he can be wholly hidden in the universe
if he so chooses, just as a child playing hide-and-go-seek can
hide himself from his playmates. Again, such a god can be
wholly revealed; his being is not inexhaustible and
incomprehensible, and he can appear wholly before men. For
such a faith, man's system and God's system must be one
system, one plan, and they must have an identity. But, since
neither is truly creator, this hope is absurd. The demand is for
a common system,

> But this identity cannot be attained. Even God has no
> absolute system. There is no such system. Reality is open.
> Time is ultimate. Chance is one of the ingredients of
> ultimate reality. The universe or Reality is *open* as well as
> closed. So God is wholly hidden as well as wholly
> revealed.[10]

Not surprisingly, in such thinking, Time becomes the new
god. Given enough millennia of years, Time will perform all
miracles and create all worlds, or so it is held.[11]

The issue in epistemology is thus one of ultimate authority.
Either man will know himself and interpret himself and the
world in terms of the word of God, or he will seek to know
himself and all things else in terms of his own ultimacy. The

---

[9.] Cornelius Van Til, *Christianity and Barthianism* (Philadelphia: Presbyterian and
Reformed Publishing Co., 1962).

[10.] *Ibid.*, 118.

[11.] See R. J. Rushdoony, *The Mythology of Science* (Nutley, N. J.: The Craig Press,
1967).

omnipotent God of Scripture has a character, an absolute nature, and therefore a predestinating decree which gives a law-structure to all reality. The autonomous man has being and no essence, for to admit to a pre-established nature is to surrender autonomy. Having no essence, and his essence or nature when he defines it being only valid for him when and where he expresses it, his word is the word of flux. Whereas God says, "I am the LORD, I change not" (Malachi 3:6), modern man must say, "I am the lord as long as I change, because to admit that any moment is superior or better than other moments is to admit a value or standard beyond myself." Christian man makes room for change, because sin must be overcome, and the earth developed under God; the realm of man, the creature, is change, but God is changeless.

10

A Valid Epistemology

It is apparent by now how deeply rooted is the cleavage between a Christian and a non-Christian epistemology. The issue is not between something more or less good on the one hand, and something very good on the other, but between mutually exclusive and irreconcilable concepts. Whether in the skepticism of Far Eastern philosophies, the idealism of the Hellenic schools, the rationalism, empiricism, Kantianism, or existentialism of modern thought, or any other non-Christian epistemology, the issue remains the same. In Van Til's telling words, "the Christian-theistic position must be shown to be not as *defensible as* some other position; it must rather be shown to be *the position which alone does not annihilate intelligent human experience.*"[1]

In view of this fact, the attempt of some churchmen to introduce autonomous man into Christian theology has only been disastrous for the faith. Two ultimates cannot co-exist unless we posit a dualism. Thus, when these thinkers introduce autonomous man into their doctrines, they effectually eliminate God.

[1.] Cornelius Van Til, *The Defense of the Faith*, 195; 1967 ed., 177.

Basic to the doctrines of orthodoxy is its conception of the absolute personal God. It holds to this doctrine as its chief and foremost constitutive concept. For Brunner, however, the idea of an absolute God is and must be nothing but a limiting conception. "For our knowledge, the Absolute is no more — though also no less — than a necessary limiting conception."[2]

When God is reduced to a limiting concept, there too man, while claiming ultimacy, is reduced to the lonely prison-house of his mind, having no world to live in except a mindless universe which is an aspect of his schizoid experience, an unhappy combination of reason with the continual experience of unreason. Autonomous man reigns in an empty and meaningless universe. As Spengler held,

> The individual may act morally or immorally, may do "good" or "evil" with respect to the primary feeling of his Culture, but the theory of his actions is not a result but a datum. Each Culture possesses its own standards, the validity of which begins and ends with it. There is no general morale of humanity.[3]

If man makes himself his own ultimate and his final reference point, then the world and knowledge are dependent upon man. Nothing exists beyond autonomous man as a reference point above and beyond him, because man is now his own god. What the unbeliever calls his epistemic point of view the Bible declares to be man's original sin (Genesis 3:1-5).

In a Christian epistemology, as we have seen, man lives by and under the absolute authority of the sovereign God. He sees God, not as an object of knowledge, but as the necessary presupposition to all knowledge. Thus, the Christian thinker does not try to "prove" the existence of God. God is not another object among a universe of objects and facts which man is trying to know, but the Creator of man and all factuality, so that all things were made by Him and are to be

---

2. Cited from Brunner, *The Philosophy of Religion*, 65f, in Cornelius Van Til, *The New Modernism* (Philadelphia: Presbyterian and Reformed Publishing Co., 1946), 173.

3. Oswald Spengler, *The Decline of the West* (New York: Knopf, [1926] 1932), I, 345.

known in terms of Him. God's self-attesting word gives us the premises for knowledge.

This does not mean, as Van Til points out, that we consult our Bible rather than go to Africa to study African animal life. The facts of life in Africa, in every form, are aspects of a world of facts which are related to one another in a way that only the Biblical presupposition with respect to all factuality makes clear. "The Bible does not claim to offer a rival theory that may or may not be true. It claims to have the ultimate *truth* about all facts."[4]

The Bible is *not* a substitute for scientific research and study but rather provides the necessary presupposition for all coherent study. Facts have meaning precisely because there is an ultimate law-order which not only is the source of all things but also the source of their coherence. "In other words, only Christian facts are possible,"[5] i.e., only in terms of Biblical faith can we account logically for the existence and coherence of factuality. Facts are theistic facts and derive their meaning from their God-ordained purpose and coherence. The Christian approach is thus neither *a priori* nor *a posteriori* but *transcendental.* "It is the firm conviction of every epistemologically self-conscious Christian-theist that no human being can utter a single syllable, whether in negation or in affirmation, unless it were for God's existence. Thus the transcendental argument seeks to discover what sort of foundations the house of human knowledge must have, in order to be what it is."[6] The transcendental argument presupposes the independence of God from the world, and the absolute dependence of the world upon God.

This fact of dependence, and the fact of sin, rule out the possibility of *neutrality* on the part of any human being. Neither the mind of man nor any aspect of his being can be independent or neutral with respect to God. God being the

---

4. Cornelius Van Til, *A Survey of Christian Epistemology* (Nutley, N. J.: Presbyterian and Reformed Publishing Co., 1969), 124.
5. *Ibid.,* 8.
6. *Ibid.,* 11.

maker of all things, there is not a neutral or independent atom in the universe. The myth of intellectual neutrality is a most dangerous belief. It presupposes that the mind of man has an autonomy or independence whereby it can view God and the universe God has created with an "objective" and "impartial" intellectual interest and with a radical neutrality. Such an assumption makes a god out of man and views him as a radical outsider to God and creation, viewing the universe merely with a remote intellectual curiosity.

The myth of neutrality puts man on an equality with God, at the very least, and, in fact, of superiority, in that a belief concomitant to neutrality is that of *the priority of time* to eternity. The determination of nature and history, and of man as well, is transferred from the eternal decree of God to time, and, eventually, into the hands of man. Man, as an aspect of his neutrality, assumes a god-like authority and a power to determine. He may ascribe determination to nature (as witness the doctrine of evolution), but he can also hold that man can now control his evolution, guide the evolution of the creation around him, and progressively control and determine the development of nature as well as history in terms of man's sovereign decree and plan.

The doctrine of *creation* asserts the priority of God and eternity to man and time. By declaring that God made all things out of nothing in the space of six days, it very baldly and plainly sets forth the divine determination of all things and the epistemological significance of God and His word. Time and eternity are separate and distinct; eternity controls time. The two are never in union outside of the person of Jesus Christ, in whom they are united without confusion or intermixture. Priority in all things belongs to eternity, to the triune God. Attempts as in Plato to bring man into relationship or union with eternity, eternal ideas, leads to an ascription to man of a divine ultimacy.

The doctrine of the *Trinity* is basic to epistemology, for without the Trinity there is no solution to the problem of the one and the many. The problem of unity or oneness as against the many or particularity has always haunted epistemology. Either the world is one, and differentiation between fact and fact is rendered difficult or meaningless, or it is many, i.e., an ocean of brute facts without any connection between one another. Philosophy has been unable to reconcile the one and the many, and only in the doctrine of the ontological Trinity do we have the equal ultimacy of the one and the many, a unity of created and uncreated reality and also their particularity.[7] "One who embraces the doctrine of the Trinity holds that human knowledge is analogical. One who does not embrace the doctrine of the Trinity holds that human knowledge is *original*."[8] The Trinity thus provides the basis for the principles of unity and diversity in human knowledge, so that knowledge can be made possible by the relationship of facts to facts without their destruction.

A corollary from the doctrine of the Trinity is that human knowledge is *analogical*. Human knowledge must always depend upon divine knowledge. Anything that a human being knows must first have been known to God. Anything a human being knows he knows only because he knows God. For that reason too man can never know anything as well and as exhaustively as God knows it.

The fact that man's knowledge must always remain analogical is applicable to his knowledge of God as well as to his knowledge of the universe. God will never be exhaustively understood in his essence by man. If he were, he would no longer be God. In that case there would be no solution for the problem of knowledge.

A third corollary from the doctrine of the Trinity is that man's knowledge though analogical is nevertheless true. Or to put it more specifically, man's knowledge is true *because* it is analogical. It is analogical because God's being unites within itself the ultimate unity and the ultimate plurality spoken of above. And it is true because there is such a God who unites this ultimate unity and plurality.

[7.] See R. J. Rushdoony, *The One and the Many* (Nutley N. J.: The Craig Press, 1971).
[8.] Cornelius Van Til, *op. cit.*, 49.

Hence we may also say that only analogical knowledge can be true knowledge.[9]

Another important consideration in epistemology is that man is now "noetically abnormal,"[10] i.e., his mind has been deflected from its created purpose by sin. In all his being, intellectually and morally, man is at war with God and separated from Him. This noetic abnormality conditions man's epistemology. For man to want a clear view of reality, i.e., to see himself and the world in the light of God, is to condemn himself in terms of God's law, and this man will not do apart from the grace of God.

But, some will hold, talk of grace is well and good with respect to our salvation. We are indeed saved by the sovereign grace of God, and we have no intention of forgetting that fact. Epistemology, however, is another area, these men hold; here we are talking about intellectual concerns, scientific research, and philosophical inquiry. To introduce grace into a context separate from redemption is, these men insist, an illegitimate extension of the idea of grace. Van Til, however, points out the unity of intellectual and soteriological approaches to the triune God:

> If one maintains that he can approach Christ of his own accord even if he is a sinner, he may as well say that he can approach the Father too. And if one can say that he knows what the fact of sin means without the enlightenment of the Holy Spirit, he may as well say that he can know other facts without reference to God. In fact he may as well say that he can know any and every fact without reference to God. If one fact can be known without reference to God there is no good reason not to hold that all facts can be known without reference to God. When the elephant of naturalism once has his nose in the door, he will not be satisfied until he is all the way in.[11]

---

9. *Ibid.*, 48.
10. *Ibid.*, 51.
11. *Ibid.*, 77.

This course of development is exactly what Arminianism in the church has manifested. By asserting an element of freedom from God for man, by weakening or abandoning the concept of God's eternal decree, it opens the door to the priority of man. For Arminianism, man can change the course of events independently of God. "Arminian theology attributes to man such powers as to enable him to do things that were not in the plan of God."[12] It in effect pictures God in heaven biting His fingernails in anxiety, waiting to see whether men will decide for or against Him. Priority is transferred from eternity to time and from God to man. The world is not under God's control but man's, and man determines the future either independently of God or in a gracious cooperation with God. The choice and determination in either case are man's.

There are, however, no facts, including the facts of sin and redemption, or intellectual decision and analysis, apart from the plan of God or His control and determination. To say this is to say that God is God; but, for many, to say that God is God is tantamount to saying that He is a monster because He will not allow man to rule or to prevail. Such people insist that man must have exclusive responsibility, whereas for Biblical faith man's responsibility, freedom, and causality are secondary. All facts are created facts, including every fact of man's history and morality. To hold that man is not man unless he can be God is neither Biblical nor logical. This in effect is the argument of Arminianism when it seeks an independence of man from the plan of God. To ensure that independence, however, it must then separate all of reality from the government of God and grant to anti-theism its fundamental principle, the irrelevance of God, whether He exists or not.

Because the reverse is true, and nothing is independent of God, certain important consequences for knowledge ensue. As Van Til has stated it,

---

12. *Ibid.*, 83.

If the Persons of the Trinity are representationally
exhaustive of one another, human thought is cast on
representational lines too. There would in that case be no
other than a completely personalistic atmosphere in
which human personality could function. Accordingly,
when man faced any fact whatsoever, he would *ipso facto*
be face to face with God. It is metaphysically as well as
religiously true that man must live and cannot but live
coram deo always. Even the meeting of one finite
personality with another finite personality would not be
truly personal if there were an impersonal atmosphere
surrounding either or both of these personalities. What
makes their meeting completely personal is the fact that
the personality of each and of both is surrounded by the
personality of God. Hence also every personal relationship
between finite persons must be mediated through the
central personality of God. Hence also every personal
relationship among men must be representational of God.
Every act of a finite person must in the nature of the case
be representational *because the only alternative to this is that
it should be completely impersonal.* We may even say that
every act of the infinite personality of God must be
representational because the only alternative to it would
be that it should be impersonal. The Trinity exists
necessarily in the manner that it does. We have seen this to
be so because the principles of unity and diversity must be
equally original. Accordingly, when we come to the
question of the nature of finite personality it is not a
handicap to finite personality to think of itself as related in
some way to the personality of God. On the contrary, the
triune God of Scripture, the internally complete
personality of God, is the very condition of its existence.
A finite personality could function in none other than a
completely personalistic atmosphere, and such an
atmosphere can be supplied to him only if his existence
depends entirely upon the exhaustive personality of
God.[13]

Unlike Kant, a Christian theory of knowledge does not
separate knowledge and faith as contradictory. Rather, they are
complimentary. Machen wrote that "it is impossible to have

---

13. *Ibid.*, 97.

faith in a person without having knowledge of the person; far from being contrasted with knowledge, faith is founded upon knowledge."[14] This knowledge is the inescapable knowledge of God, for all factuality and every fiber of man's being is revelatory of God. We, because of sin, are unwilling to acknowledge this revelation and hold it down in unrighteousness (Romans 1:18-21). By grace, we are made open to that knowledge; we believe in order that we may understand, so that, in a very real sense, knowledge is founded upon faith, in that it is faith that opens up to us that suppressed knowledge.

The approach of the Christian must be, as Van Til points out, "to reduce our opponent's position to an absurdity."[15] We must press home to the unbeliever the implications of his position and its roots in faith, a false faith, a trust in the supposed autonomy of man's mind. Any position other than the Christian theistic epistemology is trapped in impossibilities and an inability to account for the ordinary aspects of "naive realism."

> In this connection we must also say a word about the contention often made by Christians that we must be positive rather than negative in our presentation of the truth to those who have not yet accepted it. We have no fault to find with this statement if it be correctly understood. We must certainly present the truth of the Christian theistic system constantly, at every point of the argument. But it is clear that if you offer a new wife to one who is perfectly satisfied with the one he has now, you are not likely to be relieved of your burden. In other words, it is the self-sufficiency of the "natural man" that must first be brought under some pressure, before there is any likelihood of his even considering the truth in any serious fashion at all. The parable of the prodigal son helps us here. As long as the son was at home there was nothing but a positive argument that was held before him. But he wanted to go out of the father's house in order to indulge in "riotous living." Not till he was at the swinetrough, not

---

14. J. Gresham Machen, *What is Faith?* (Grand Rapids: Eerdmans, 1946), 46.
15. Cornelius Van Til, *Survey of Christian Epistemology*, 205.

till he saw that he had made a hog of himself and that he could not be a hog because he was a man, did he at all begin to consider the servants of his father who had plenty of bread. The kingdom of God must be built upon the destruction of the enemy.[16]

Few better ways of destroying the enemy exist than by a rigorous use of the Christian theory of knowledge, by pointing out to men that, on their anti-theistic epistemologies, they "annihilate intelligent human experience." On the argument of presupposition, the premises of anti-theistic thought can be unmasked as the absurdities they are, and the sovereign God set forth as the only valid presupposition for a tenable theory of knowledge.

16. *Ibid.*, 207.

11

The Flight From Reality

Let us again ask the question, "What is the significance of epistemology?," so that we can examine a very practical facet of the problem. If the average man were told that a major problem of philosophy in the modern era was to account for the reality of the external world, or that philosophers felt that the existence of things "out there," outside our minds, is unprovable, he would conclude that the philosophers were "crazy" and that philosophy is an absurd discipline.

There would be two serious errors in such a reaction. *First,* there would be a failure to appreciate the calibre and ability of the philosophers, and their honesty in pursuing their presupposition as far as they have. *Second,* there would be a failure to appreciate how deeply this same philosophy has influenced virtually all modern men. "The man on the street" is a product of modern epistemology.

Medieval and Reformation men, as they looked out at the world, whatever the defects of either, still saw the universe as a God-given, God-created reality, and they saw themselves as *a part* of that reality.

Modern man, however, has been differently schooled. The implications of his epistemology are very clear: *reality is a part of me*.

The consequences of such an attitude are far-reaching. They do lead to a flight from reality. If the belief that reality in some sense is an aspect of our consciousness, and has its "existence" as a state of mind, is held, then man will be more concerned about his states of mind that about God and the world.

Not surprisingly, *fiction* has played a more central part in modern culture than in any previous society. It has transformed daily life and popular culture. Thus, in the medieval era, music had as its major expression the music of the church, sung to the glory of God and man's joy in Him. Popular music reflected everyday life. Romantic love became important in certain kinds of music late in that era.

Modern music began as a background to royal courts, and was designed to make more congenial the royal courts and to facilitate fantasy and pleasure. All the great modern composers of the earlier era, and with some, like Wagner, well into the nineteenth century, lived on royal patronage. Their music provided the liturgy of the court, designed to convey the majesty, divinity, and harmony of royal life as a background to the court's activities. Opera carried fantasy further: wild heroics placed man in a dream world wherein portentous consequences hung on every word and act of a man and a maid.

The heroic play, tragedy, and various other forms of drama again stressed the grand role of man and his greatness even in defeat. Novels soon became popular, one of the most, if not the most, popular medium in all the history of art, and relying on a taste for fiction and an identification with persons of diverse kinds.

The twentieth century, however, has seen the triumph of fiction, and also of revolution, which is an attempt to make fantasy real. Modern man now gets a diet of a few hours daily of a dream world via motion pictures and television. Women often are surrounded by the fictions of television all day.

The cults of modern man, religious and otherwise, again thrive on fantasy. The world has ceased to be more than an image in our imagination, for all too many people. A popular answer to questions expressing doubts about some measure is, "Well, the government will do something about it before it happens," or, "Someone will come up with an answer." In brief, reality will bend to man's imagination. There is no belief in a day of reckoning with reality, let alone a belief in the day of judgment.

Scientists, we are assured, will reverse the aging process and make the old young again. The next step, we are told, is "Homo deus."[1]

This is no longer a belief that the entrepreneur will work to overcome problems but rather a belief in wish fulfillment, a faith that reality will bend to the imagination of man. Therefore, the counsel is, "Hold a good thought." When monetary crises developed in the 1960s and 1970s, there were more than a few who turned on those who had forecast these things to blame them for it; all would have been well but for their negative thinking. "The power of positive thinking" had come to represent the implicit faith of modern man. A president like John F. Kennedy was widely admired and idolized because he said and believed the "right" things while bumbling on confrontation with reality; his thought-world somehow created "Camelot" for the world of scholars and politicians as well as millions of Americans.

The radio and television keep man bathed in a dream world, and what they do not supply, his imagination does. The sexual revolution has deep roots in this flight from reality, in dreams of a consequence-free world of perpetual youth.

In brief, modern man is a product of his epistemology. He lives in a dream world, implicitly believing that reality is somehow, or will be somehow, a part of man, and totally at

---

[1] Saul-Paul Sirag, "Scientists now working on reversing aging process," in the Los Angeles *Free Press*, 10, 8 (February 23, 1973), 3.

the command of man's imagination some day. His awakening will be a rude one, and God will be in it.

Appendix 1

Bootstrap Reasoning

In an entirely different context than epistemology, Heller has raised a very pertinent point with respect of the problem of definition:

> Barring pathological complications such as the loss of the sense of taste, anyone who has ever tasted strawberry recognizes its characteristic flavor and would never confuse it, say, with vanilla or chocolate or lemon. Yet no one has ever succeeded in *defining* the taste of strawberry in a useful way, one subject to the restriction indicated.[1]

In other words, proof is impossible, unless a prior knowledge-experience context exists, with so simple a thing as the taste of strawberries. It is then not so much a proof as a development of circular reasoning. We can then *define* the taste of strawberries only to someone who has tasted strawberries and knows what they are like. By appealing to that taste of strawberries, we can raise questions about artificial strawberry flavorings, and we can judge that this particular flavoring comes closer to the authentic strawberry flavor than another.

[1.] L. G. Heller, *The Death of the American University* (New Rochelle, N.Y.: Arlington House, 1973).

Knowledge rests on knowledge. The idea that a man can begin with total ignorance and work his way to knowledge has serious problems. The correlation, the awareness of structure and parallels, and the ability to utilize data which constitute learning rest on prior knowledge. None of us is born into ignorance. Even as newborn babes, we enter into a language and knowledge continuum and a total world of people and history which sets a pattern upon us before we are aware that such things exist.

When a man tries to begin, as philosophy has since Descartes, entirely devoid of all knowledge and with nothing save existence, the existence of the subjective individual, the consequence is cultural loss. Knowledge disappears, and ignorance prevails. If there is no strawberry flavor until we *prove* that there is, and define what it is, and if we must do this *before* we acknowledge the existence of either strawberries or a strawberry flavor, we get nowhere. The impasse of modern philosophy is a product of its idea of beginning with bare subjective existence and building outward from there. Instead, existence itself becomes dubious.

Nothing is known unless there is first the presupposition of knowledge, and on no other ground is such a presupposition possible than the Christian theistic one. We *know* a real world because we believe by faith that God created it. From our first breath as a babe, we assume the reality of that world and the trustworthiness of our knowledge and experience.

When the logic of the fall develops in us, we deny that knowledge, because it points to God and the revelation the fall challenges. As a result, the fallen man as philosopher must challenge and question the knowledge he took for granted as a child.

On the other hand, covenant man realizes progressively how that world of knowledge rests on God. "Through faith we understand that the worlds were framed by the word of God, so that things which are seen were not made of things which do appear" (Heb. 11:3). Because man is created in God's image,

even though that image is under the effects of the fall, the fact
remains that God's image, as does all His creation, witnesses to
God. As St. Paul declared, "That which may be known of God
is manifest in them, for God hath shewed it unto them" (Rom.
1:19; in the Berkeley Version, this reads, "whatever can be
known regarding God is evident to them, for God has shown
it to them").

Man created in the image of God is able to have knowledge
because he is born into a world of meaning has himself a
meaning; he signifies something in terms of God's purpose and
decree. He is born into a context of knowledge as a central
strand therein, and not even the baleful influence of sin can
entirely destroy that context for him. The inescapable
knowledge of God, and the unity of the creation under God,
is evident to man, however much he suppresses it because of
his unrighteousness (Rom. 1:18-19). The English version of
1880 for Romans 1:8-10 reads, "For the wrath of God is
revealed   from   heaven   against   all   ungodliness   and
unrighteousness of men, who hold down the truth in
unrighteousness; because that which may be known of God is
manifest in them; for God manifested it to them."

Definition in a world of brute factuality is an impossibility.
There is no common universe for factuality, no eternal decree
as the frame of reference, and no ground whatsoever for any
analogy. Each brute fact is its own universe and its own
meaning. It cannot be defined or described by the meaning or
language of any other fact without an implicit denial of the
idea of brute factuality. Definition implies an eternal decree.
Without that eternal decree and with only brute factuality,
knowledge is impossible.

Definition and knowledge in God's world are possible
because both particularity and universality exist. All things are
part of a seamless garment as a result of God's eternal decree of
predestination. All things point to all things else as an aspect of
their context and meaning. At the same time, each fact has its
specific and unique meaning as a particular and cannot be
reduced to a formless drop in a ocean of nothingness. Each fact

has its particular place and meaning in God's sight, so that knowledge is assured by the reality of both particularity and universality.

The kind of thinking done by philosophers from Descartes to the present, in the modern tradition, can be called *bootstrap reasoning*. No more than a man can raise himself off the ground by tugging as his bootstraps can a man, on the premise of autonomous reason, go beyond his own existence. Every attempt to reason apart from the presupposition of the triune God and His infallible word ends logically in bootstrap reasoning.

Appendix 2

A Note on Recent Developments in Epistemology

Having accepted modern philosophy, scientists of the 20th century are amazed that their mathematics works, that calculations can put a man on the moon with accuracy and assurance. Thus, Dr. Remo J. Ruffini, a physicist at Princeton University, has observed:

> How a mathematical structure can correspond to nature is a mystery. One way out is just to say that the language in which nature speaks is the language of mathematics. This begs the question. Often we are both shocked and surprised by the correspondence between mathematics and nature, especially when the experiment confirms that our mathematical model describes nature perfectly.

> This surprise and shock automatically pose a different question, which some people choose to answer in a religious manner and others refuse to even ask. At this point the decision involves recognizing the presence of a god who has arranged it all. To some people the question does not make sense.... After pulsar (stars that have undergone partial gravitational collapse and are emitting light in sharply defined pulses — also called neutron stars) were discovered, I spoke with Emelio Segre, who was awarded the Nobel Prize for his discovery of the

antiproton. I told him we were finally convinced that we had found neutron stars. And Segre, speaking in elegant, old-fashioned Italian, said, "Perhaps God is so powerful that He could find a different way of making a pulsar than a neutron star. How can you be so definite in saying you have found a neutron star?" He was alluding, I think, to the problem of the theoretician, which is not just to find *a* correspondence between his theoretical frame work and the physical world but to find the *unique* correspondence.[1]

Correspondence between logic and factuality in a world of chance variations is indeed a cause for "shock" and "mystery." Since Kant, philosophy has been committed to the autonomy and ultimacy of man's mind, but it has not been able to forget that things in themselves are out there and are somehow to be explained. As Reck has observed (in a discussion of C. S. Lewis), "Plagued with explaining the uniformity of nature, and finding none, empiricists have nonetheless continued the rule of induction from past to future experience. They have proceeded with practical correctness but without theoretical justification."[2] The fact of correlation and correspondence is recognized; some, like F. C. S. Northrop, have named the process "an epistemic correlation," but they have not thereby given us any valid reason for it in terms of their presuppositions.

Much earlier, Thomas Reid (1710-1796) opposed Hume's epistemological skepticism with his Common Sense philosophy or the doctrine of Presentative Realism. For this school, objects in the outer world are presented to the consciousness directly, not through an intermediate process of sensations, so that, instead of a second-hand impression, the mind has a direct contact with the real object itself. However this in itself led to a problem, as Sahakian notes:

...No distinction is to be drawn between what a thing seems to be and what it is in reality, since nothing

---

[1.] "The Princeton Galaxy," Interviews by Florence Heltizer, in *Intellectual Digest* III, 10 (June, 1973), 27.

[2.] Andres J. Reck, *The New American Philosophers, An Exploration of Thought Since World War II* (New York: Delta, [1968] 1970), 24.

intervenes between the knower and the object of his knowledge (the external world of reality).

But if real objects are precisely identical with our perceptions of them, how could there be any possibility of perceptual error?[3]

The implication of such a position is the infallibility of man's mind, but it is still a dubious infallibility, in that it requires a link a dependence on the external world of reality. This link some recent philosophers have severed. The principle of the fall, that truth must be abstracted and separated from God, is now carried further. First, truth was recognized, in terms of Scripture, as inseparable from God. Truth is what God says, does, is, and ordains. God and His words and works cannot be judged by an abstract criterion of truth, because God is truth in all His being. Second, truth was abstracted from God and made a common pursuit of God and man. Both can know the truth or fall short of the truth. Truth is associated either with abstract ideas, or with the facts of the external world. In either case, it is separate from God and man. Third, after Kant, truth has been more and more closely identified with the mind of man, as in existentialism, so that a new infallibility, without any external frame of reference and similar to the Biblical doctrine of God's infallibility, is affirmed. Truth is what man is and does and "doing your own thing," the hippy standard of the 1960s, is affirming yourself as ultimacy and truth.

In such a perspective, science is at least irrelevant, and knowledge really means self-knowledge. The consequence is the collapse of society and the bankruptcy of philosophy.

[3.] William S. Sahakian, *History of Philosophy* (New York: Barnes & Noble, [1968] 1970), 289.

Appendix 3

A Systematic Anthropology?

The denial of God's sovereignty and His predestination is the denial of systematic theology. God having no pre-established plan, law, and pattern in and over the universe, no system or pattern exists in the universe, it is held, whereby a systematic body of doctrine can be deduced. We have instead only brute factuality.

Systematic theology is denied in order to replace it with a systematic anthropology. The predestination, planning, and control of God is set aside to be replaced by the predestination, planning, and control of the new sovereign, man, or of man's agency, the scientific socialist state. The result has been, in the modern era, a series of attempts to create a systematic anthropology.

One of the more prominent efforts at a systematic anthropology is Marxism, a militant and dedicated form of humanism. The contempt Marx expressed for religion and metaphysics is well known; it is also increasingly recognized that Marx's viewpoint was an intensely religious humanism and that metaphysical presuppositions governed his total viewpoint. Moreover, Marx found it necessary to sneak more than a little systematic theology into his philosophy. Thus, a

121

decree of predestination was assumed and called the dialectical process, and, to make sure that it would not be confused with Biblical faith, it was aggressively termed dialectical materialism. This decree of Marxist predestination works above and beyond man to create the triumph of the proletariat revolution. This triumph is inevitable because it is an aspect of this decree or predestination. It is a purposive, selective, and irreversible decree, so that Marx posits the God of Scripture while denying Him. This fact is concealed under the term "dialectical materialism." Marx's God controls all factors and presses every button while being carefully concealed in a philosophical closet. Once Marx's God achieves the established goal, the triumph of the proletariat, He fades even further into the background, allowing man the privilege of establishing a humanistic decree and paradise while He, in the shadows, assures its smooth operation. Marx's systematic anthropology turns out to be a systematic theology wearing a mask. We should not be surprised, as the Marxist world falters and decays, to see its citizens move either towards a form of Calvinism, or, in disillusionment, to a most radical form of nihilism.

Existentialism more logically finds itself unable to construct a systematic anthropology. Man has existence, but no essence, no pattern of nature, and hence no natural or inherent decree. God's sovereignty is an aspect of His being, so that, because God is God, He creates, predestines, and absolutely controls all things: there is nothing apart from Him. For existentialism, there is no identity between existence and essence. For man, *to be* does not necessarily mean *to create, predestine,* and *govern.* In fact, man is born of woman, as a helpless child, and only slowly learns to control the most elementary functions of his body. Man's aspirations *can* be to be a god, but this does not mean that he is one. Moreover, in existentialism, there is nothing in common between man and man except existence, and no systematics can be constructed on the bare fact of existence. All that can be said is that *man is*, but it must be added that, *man may not be, for man can die*. Not even man's existence is thus any ground for a systematics. The pattern man establishes today for himself, as his own private universe, can disintegrate tomorrow with a change of heart, for mutability marks man's days, or with his death. Existentialist man is indeed "a futile passion," and a systematic anthropology is an impossibility.

Appendix 4

The Lack of Epistemological Self-Consciousness

The notable and marked lack of epistemological self-consciousness which marks the modern humanistic scientific establishment is very sharply illustrated by Weston La Barre, professor of anthropology at Duke University, especially in his work, *The Ghost Dance, Origins of Religion* (1970). What purports to account scientifically for religion is a militant attack on it. The temper of the book appears in the dedication:

> To my Fathers
> of the flesh and of the spirit
> who posed me these problems
> and to Jean-Francois Lefebvre
> Chevalier de La Barre
> burned at the stake in Abbeville
> 1 July 1766 at the age of eighteen.[1]

In this spirit, La Barre proceeds with the emphatic determination to burn the idea of supernatural religion at the stake of "science." The first paragraph of his "Preface" declares:

> This book is a psychological and anthropological study in religion. Naturalistically approached, human religion

---

[1.] Weston La Barre, *The Ghost Dance, Origins of Religion* (Garden City, N.Y.: Doubleday & Company, 1970), vii.

turns out to be an *entirely* human phenomenon, and
entirely derived from the nature of human nature.
Religion has never been explainable in the terms provided
by religion, and the long search for knowledge of the gods
or of God has given us no knowledge whatever that is
acceptable to all men. Why not then look carefully at man
himself for an understanding of this human
phenomenon?[2]

Let us analyze this statement from the standpoint of
Christianity. What La Barre is saying is that no evidence will
be considered, and nothing will be deemed admissible as
evidence, *unless* it is naturalistic. On this premise, quite
logically, the only evidence present is naturalistic and shows
religion to be an *"entirely* human product." After all, if we rule
out beforehand every and any consideration of the reality of
Biblical religion, then it follows that it can give us "no
knowledge whatever that is acceptable to all men." (Of course,
La Barre's "evidence" is also not "acceptable to all men," but it
is obvious by "all men" that La Barre admits only men like
himself into standing as men!) A more naive epistemological
statement than this paragraph by La Barre, especially the
second sentence, is difficult to imagine.

Let us alter the application a bit to make clear the
implications of La Barre's position. If we determine
beforehand that, the only way to understand Weston La Barre,
John Doe, the reader, and myself is as psychopaths, then the
only existing evidence possible concerning our natures is
predetermined to show us to be psychopaths. This is not
science but a form of intellectual burning at the stake of
unpopular persons or ideas.

Epistemological self-consciousness is needed to preserve us
from objectifying our limitations and prejudices into a
"science" or "philosophy." This is precisely what is lacking in
the modern world. Men's limitations have become their
standards, and their yardsticks legislate their errors into
science. A truly Biblical epistemology will be aware of its

---

2. *Ibid.*

limitations and aware also of the impossibility of gaining exhaustive knowledge. Exhaustive knowledge is a legitimate humanistic goal; for the Christian, it is an impossible and illegitimate goal, and this imposes a necessary humility on him. (Too commonly, Christianity has been governed by Aristotelian or neoplatonic epistemologies, and hence singularly lacking in the Christian grace of humility.) Moreover, the fact that, for the Christian, true knowledge must be grounded on revelation, and this fact is a judgment on the supposed autonomy and ultimacy of human rationality. Where revelation governs man's epistemology, it means that the world is undergirded by the certainties of God, but man's realm and reason cannot claim the same certainties. Epistemology then is a recognition of the limitations as well as the real powers of human knowledge, as well as a self-conscious recognition of the presuppositions inescapable to all knowledge.

Scripture Index

Index

The Author

Rousas John Rushdoony (1916-2001) was a well-known American scholar, writer, and author of over thirty books. He held B.A. and M.A. degrees from the University of California and received his theological training at the Pacific School of Religion. An ordained minister, he worked as a missionary among Paiute and Shoshone Indians as well as a pastor to two California churches. He founded the Chalcedon Foundation, an educational organization devoted to research, publishing, and cogent communication of a distinctively Christian scholarship to the world at large. His writing in the *Chalcedon Report* and his numerous books spawned a generation of believers active in reconstructing the world to the glory of Jesus Christ. He resided in Vallecito, California until his death, where he engaged in research, lecturing, and assisting others in developing programs to put the Christian Faith into action.

The Ministry of Chalcedon

CHALCEDON (kal•see•don) is a Christian educational organization devoted exclusively to research, publishing, and cogent communication of a distinctively Christian scholarship to the world at large. It makes available a variety of services and programs, all geared to the needs of interested ministers, scholars, and laymen who understand the propositions that Jesus Christ speaks to the mind as well as the heart, and that His claims extend beyond the narrow confines of the various institutional churches. We exist in order to support the efforts of all orthodox denominations and churches. Chalcedon derives its name from the great ecclesiastical Council of Chalcedon (A.D. 451), which produced the crucial Christological definition: "Therefore, following the holy Fathers, we all with one accord teach men to acknowledge one and the same Son, our Lord Jesus Christ, at once complete in Godhead and complete in manhood, truly God and truly man...." This formula directly challenges every false claim of divinity by any human institution: state, church, cult, school, or human assembly. Christ alone is both God and man, the unique link between heaven and earth. All human power is therefore derivative: Christ alone can announce that "All power is given unto me in heaven and in earth" (Matthew 28:18). Historically, the Chalcedonian creed is therefore the foundation of Western liberty, for it sets limits on all authoritarian human institutions by acknowledging the validity of the claims of the One who is the source of true human freedom (Galatians 5:1).

The *Chalcedon Report* is published monthly and is sent to all who request it. All gifts to Chalcedon are tax deductible.

Chalcedon
Box 158
Vallecito, CA 95251 U.S.A.
www.chalcedon.edu